CHARLOTTE TILBURY

Her Life and Legacy, From Makeup Artist to Global Beauty Icon — A Biography

Santos M. Martinez

Charlotte Tilbury biography

Copyright © [2025] by [Santos M. Martinez]

All rights reserved.

No part of this publication may be reproduced, stored in a retrieval system, or transmitted in any form or by any means—electronic, mechanical, photocopying, recording, or otherwise—without prior written permission from the publisher, except in the case of brief quotations used in critical articles, academic work, or legally permitted uses under applicable copyright law.

This book is a work of original nonfiction authorship. While it draws on publicly available sources to document real individuals and events, the structure, interpretation, composition, and presentation of facts reflect the author's independent research and creative discretion.

Every effort has been made to ensure the accuracy and completeness of the information provided. The author and publisher disclaim liability for any errors, omissions, or interpretations arising from source material or evolving public records.

Charlotte Tilbury biography

Disclaimer

This book is an independent, unauthorized biography. It is not affiliated with, endorsed by, sponsored by, or officially connected to the individual profiled, their family, representatives, estate, or any related entity.

The content is based entirely on publicly available information, reliable sources, and independent research. All interpretations, context, and narrative decisions are those of the author.

Names, likenesses, and references to individuals or organizations are used solely for descriptive and editorial purposes. Trademarks and registered marks, if mentioned, remain the property of their respective owners.

This work is intended for informational and educational purposes. If any individual or organization believes any part of this book infringes on their rights, they are encouraged to contact the publisher for a timely and good-faith resolution.

Charlotte Tilbury biography

TABLE OF CONTENTS

INTRODUCTION 6
PART I: ORIGINS AND EARLY INSPIRATIONS 13
    Chapter 1: Childhood in London and Ibiza 14
    Chapter 2: Entering the World of Beauty 23
PART II: ESTABLISHING A MAKEUP CAREER 31
    Chapter 3: From London to the Fashion Runways 32
    Chapter 4: Collaborations with Photographers and Models 40
    Chapter 5: British Vogue and Editorial Influence 49
PART III: BECOMING A PUBLIC BEAUTY AUTHORITY 58
    Chapter 6: Breakthrough as a Celebrity Makeup Artist 59
    Chapter 7: Industry Recognition and Awards 69
    Chapter 8: From Makeup Chair to Global Stage 79
PART IV: BUILDING CHARLOTTE TILBURY BEAUTY 88
    Chapter 9: Founding the Brand in 2013 89
    Chapter 10: Product Icons and Bestsellers 98
    Chapter 11: Global Expansion and Flagship Stores 111
    Chapter 12: Accolades and Industry Partnerships 123

PART V: LEADERSHIP, AMBASSADORSHIP, AND INFLUENCE — 137

Chapter 13: Beauty Advocate and Industry Ambassador — 138
Chapter 14: Digital Strategy and Modern Marketing — 148
Chapter 15: Philanthropy and Social Responsibility — 162

PART VI: PERSONAL DIMENSIONS — 175

Chapter 16: Life Beyond the Brand — 176
Chapter 17: Charlotte Tilbury as a Cultural Icon — 188

PART VII: PRESENT DAY AND THE FUTURE — 201

Chapter 18: The 2020s Beauty Landscape — 202
Chapter 19: Acquisitions and Corporate Milestones — 215
Chapter 20: Recent Successes and Global Campaigns — 228
Chapter 21: Holiday 2025 Collection and Future Vision — 240

CONCLUSION — 253

Charlotte Tilbury biography

INTRODUCTION

There are few names in the beauty world that command immediate recognition across continents, and among them, Charlotte Tilbury stands in rare company. Known not only as a makeup artist but as a global entrepreneur who turned artistry into empire, her story bridges fashion runways, celebrity circles, and boardrooms in equal measure. What makes her journey compelling is not just the glamour of lipsticks and palettes but the determination, strategy, and cultural timing that allowed her to reshape an industry often resistant to reinvention.

Born in London and raised between the British capital and the bohemian atmosphere of Ibiza, Tilbury grew up surrounded by creativity. Her father, Lance Tilbury, was a painter, and her mother, Patsy Dodd, brought another layer of artistic energy to the household. Those early environments planted seeds that later bloomed into a brand vision defined by artistry, color, and performance. What sets her apart from many contemporaries, however, is not simply her early exposure to art, but the way she recognized beauty as both an expressive force and a commercial frontier.

By the early 1990s, Tilbury had formally trained at the Glauca Rossi School of Makeup in London, stepping into a highly competitive industry at a moment when fashion was shifting from the glossy excess of the 1980s to a grittier, editorial-driven era. She quickly learned that makeup was not only about application but about storytelling. Her backstage work at fashion weeks, on magazine shoots, and with some of the world's most celebrated photographers sharpened her technical edge. The late 1990s and early 2000s saw her establish herself as one of the leading creative figures in editorial beauty, collaborating with Mario Testino, Mert & Marcus, and stylists whose visions helped redefine modern fashion.

Her artistry became linked with some of the most recognizable faces of the era. She worked closely with Kate Moss, helping to create looks that mirrored the evolving aesthetic of the time: sultry, effortless, and strikingly modern. Tilbury's work was not confined to the anonymity of the backstage. She wrote and contributed as Beauty Editor-at-Large for *British Vogue*, extending her influence beyond brushes and pigments to shaping how millions of women thought about beauty in their everyday lives. These roles positioned her as more than a behind-the-scenes figure; she became an authority.

Yet what makes Charlotte Tilbury's ascent remarkable is her ability to leap from the personal artistry of applying makeup to the commercial reality of building one of the world's most recognizable luxury beauty brands. In 2013, she launched *Charlotte Tilbury Beauty* with its debut at Selfridges in London. The launch was a sensation, with consumers drawn to both the products themselves and the storytelling that surrounded them. Her signature Magic Cream, developed years earlier as a backstage staple, quickly became a bestseller. Lipsticks, especially the universally flattering Pillow Talk shade, cemented her reputation for creating not only trends but long-lasting icons of modern beauty.

From that point, the business grew with astonishing speed. Expansions into international markets brought her brand to the United States, the Middle East, and Asia. Partnerships with retailers such as Sephora and

Charlotte Tilbury biography

Net-a-Porter ensured accessibility across digital and physical shelves. By the late 2010s, *Charlotte Tilbury Beauty* had become synonymous with luxury, performance, and aspirational glamour. Her distinct branding—rich burgundy packaging, art deco influences, and her personal presence in marketing campaigns—made the brand instantly identifiable.

Recognition from the British establishment soon followed. In 2018, Tilbury was named a Member of the Order of the British Empire (MBE) for her services to the beauty and cosmetics industry. The honor not only acknowledged her entrepreneurial impact but also her role as a cultural ambassador for British creativity on the world stage. Two years later, her company reached another milestone when the Spanish fashion and fragrance group Puig acquired a majority stake in *Charlotte Tilbury Beauty*. This deal provided the resources for even wider global expansion while allowing Tilbury to retain her creative leadership.

Tilbury's influence has always extended beyond products. She was among the earliest major makeup artists to harness the potential of digital media, launching

Charlotte Tilbury biography

YouTube tutorials, Instagram campaigns, and influencer partnerships before many legacy beauty brands recognized their significance. In doing so, she bridged a generational gap: older consumers knew her from fashion and magazines, while younger audiences discovered her through social platforms. This strategic embrace of digital culture transformed her into not just a beauty founder but a modern marketer whose methods reshaped industry playbooks.

Her story also carries a distinctly personal layer. Known for her flame-red hair and glamorous self-presentation, Tilbury has maintained a public image that blends accessibility with mystique. She has spoken about balancing her career with motherhood, and while her personal life remains largely private, her brand narrative has always drawn from her own personality. Consumers did not just buy makeup; they bought into the world of Charlotte Tilbury—its glamour, confidence, and vision of empowerment.

In the 2020s, Tilbury's career has entered a new phase marked by adaptation to an ever-changing industry. The COVID-19 pandemic brought unprecedented challenges to beauty retail, yet her brand responded quickly with e-commerce innovation, virtual try-ons, and digital consultations. The result was sustained growth even in a period when in-store sales were collapsing globally. By 2023 and 2024, the brand had expanded its skincare line and continued to dominate conversations around luxury makeup, particularly with ongoing expansions of the Pillow Talk collection.

The pace has not slowed in 2025. In October of this year, Charlotte Tilbury unveiled her holiday products collection, a launch that combined festive artistry with the commercial sharpness her brand is known for. The release reinforced her position as a tastemaker who understands both seasonal consumer desires and the long-term positioning of luxury beauty in a competitive marketplace.

What makes her story resonate now is not only the remarkable trajectory of her career but the way it encapsulates broader shifts in culture and commerce. Charlotte Tilbury's journey reflects the merging of artistry with entrepreneurship, of individual creativity with global corporate strategy, and of tradition with digital innovation. Her life offers a lens through which to understand how the beauty industry—once confined to department store counters and magazine spreads—has become a worldwide cultural force.

To chart her rise is to understand how one woman turned personal vision into collective aspiration, how she balanced the intimacy of makeup artistry with the scale of a global enterprise, and how she redefined beauty standards for an age that demands both glamour and accessibility. Her story is about more than products or accolades; it is about vision, timing, and the persistence to transform a lifelong passion into a legacy that shows no sign of slowing down.

The following pages trace that legacy in full, from a childhood surrounded by art to a career that redefined beauty's place in fashion, business, and culture. It is a story of transformation—of an individual, of an industry, and of the ways we understand the role of beauty in modern life.

Charlotte Tilbury biography

PART I: ORIGINS AND EARLY INSPIRATIONS

Every story of transformation begins with a foundation, and Charlotte Tilbury's journey is no exception. Long before she became a household name in beauty, her life was shaped by the environments, influences, and passions of her earliest years. From the creative energy of her family to the contrasting worlds of London and Ibiza, these beginnings reveal the roots of an imagination that would one day redefine glamour. Part I traces those origins, showing how the spark of artistry was nurtured and how the first steps toward a life in beauty quietly took form.

Charlotte Tilbury biography

Chapter 1: Childhood in London and Ibiza

Charlotte Tilbury was born in London in 1973 into a family whose creative roots and bohemian outlook would come to shape her identity in profound ways. From the very beginning, her environment was steeped in art, culture, and a sense of expression that was not confined by traditional boundaries. To understand the woman who would one day transform the global beauty industry, it is essential to begin with the textures of her early life, where brushes and canvases were as familiar as books and toys, and where the visual world was never taken for granted.

Her father, Lance Tilbury, played a central role in this artistic backdrop. A painter by trade, Lance filled the family's life with color, perspective, and imagination. His work often explored form and movement, reflecting the kind of curiosity that naturally flowed into the way Charlotte experienced her surroundings. A painter's household is never ordinary, and in the Tilbury home, creative exploration was part of the daily rhythm. Paints, palettes, and canvases were more than professional tools for Lance; they were an extension of his personality, a reminder that art could filter into the smallest corners of life. For Charlotte, this was not an abstract influence. She saw creativity as a language, something her father communicated through each stroke of a brush.

Growing up in London gave Charlotte early exposure to one of the world's most dynamic cities. The 1970s in London were years of cultural experimentation, where fashion and music collided in ways that defined a generation. Even as a child, she would have been surrounded by this energy. London was not just a place where styles were worn; it was a place where they were invented, deconstructed, and reinvented again. For someone with a naturally observant eye, the city itself became an open book of inspiration. Its streets carried the buzz of subcultures, from the remnants of the swinging sixties to the emerging waves of punk and new romanticism. To grow up in this environment meant absorbing ideas that blurred the line between everyday life and performance.

Charlotte Tilbury biography

Her upbringing was not confined to London alone. The family also lived in Ibiza, an island known for its wild beauty, artistic enclaves, and unconventional spirit. The move was not a rejection of London but an expansion of the world Charlotte was coming to know. Ibiza in the 1970s and 1980s was a sanctuary for creative souls. Artists, musicians, and free thinkers gravitated to the island, creating a unique community that thrived on expression without inhibition. For a child like Charlotte, these surroundings were formative. The island's Mediterranean light, the clash of natural landscapes with bursts of color in art and fashion, and the cultural openness that defined Ibiza all left a lasting impression.

Life between London and Ibiza created a duality in Charlotte's childhood that became one of her defining traits. London gave her the structure of a cultural capital, with its galleries, theaters, and vibrant fashion scene. Ibiza, in contrast, offered her freedom, imagination, and the influence of a community where expression was not just encouraged but celebrated. These two worlds did not conflict; they complemented each other, giving Charlotte both discipline and freedom, urban energy and island creativity.

In Ibiza, her father's work as a painter took on even deeper meaning. Lance was part of the artistic community on the island, and Charlotte witnessed firsthand what it meant to live a life dedicated to creative passion. Watching him in his studio, translating inspiration into form, Charlotte absorbed an understanding that creativity was not a pastime but a way of living. Lance's example was not about technical instruction; he was not teaching her how to paint. Instead, he was showing her that art was a valid and vital pursuit, one that could shape not only a career but an entire existence.

Her mother, Patsy, also contributed to this environment, providing balance and grounding. While details of Patsy's work and influence are less publicly documented, her presence in Charlotte's upbringing created the family structure within which creativity could flourish. The household combined the artistic with the practical, giving Charlotte the sense that imagination needed space but also support. This balance of nurturing freedom while providing stability was critical to her development.

In both London and Ibiza, Charlotte was surrounded by performance and self-expression. Music was a central part of life on the island, with its reputation as a hub for nightlife and cultural experimentation. Fashion, too, was visible everywhere, whether in the couture of London's fashion weeks or in the eclectic, free-spirited styles of Ibiza's markets. As a child, she learned that appearance could be more than surface. It could be identity, mood, and art. These early exposures planted the seeds of an understanding that beauty and performance were inseparable from how people presented themselves to the world.

Charlotte's awareness of style and self-presentation grew not only from what she observed but also from how she participated. She has spoken of experimenting with makeup from a young age, fascinated by its ability to transform and elevate. These experiments were not just games of childhood curiosity; they were part of a larger exploration into how art could translate onto the human canvas. Unlike her father's canvases, which hung on walls, her interest lay in how artistry could live on faces, in motion, interacting with light and emotion.

The cultural context of her upbringing cannot be overstated. The 1970s and 1980s were decades of dramatic shifts in fashion and art. In London, the glam rock era, the rise of punk, and the emergence of designers who challenged traditional notions of beauty all created an atmosphere of change. In Ibiza, the community of artists and performers made the extraordinary feel ordinary. These influences ensured that Charlotte grew up with a sense that creativity was not distant or unattainable. It was everywhere, part of daily life, part of how people related to one another.

Her father's influence was particularly profound. Lance Tilbury's work as a painter was not about celebrity or commercial success but about dedication to the craft. He showed Charlotte that creative work required discipline, resilience, and passion. Watching him balance the demands of family life with the pursuit of art gave her a model for integrating creativity into the fabric of existence. His encouragement helped foster her confidence, showing her that artistic ambition was something to be embraced rather than hidden.

By the time she was old enough to think about her own path, Charlotte had internalized these lessons. She had seen creativity lived every day, not as a sideline but as a center. She had witnessed the ways art could be both personal and communal, both disciplined and spontaneous. Her understanding of beauty, performance, and artistry was rooted in this childhood foundation. London gave her the exposure to fashion and culture, while Ibiza gave her freedom and experimentation. And through it all, her father's example as a painter reminded her that art, in any form, was not just possible but necessary.

This combination of influences made Charlotte Tilbury's childhood unique. It was not a typical upbringing in a conventional sense, but it was precisely the kind of environment that could nurture someone destined to redefine beauty on a global scale. The contrasts and connections between her two homes, the daily immersion in art and performance, and the guiding presence of her father all created the foundation for the vision she would later bring to the world.

Charlotte Tilbury's childhood was not marked by the pursuit of fame or fortune but by immersion in creativity. It was a time of discovery, of learning to see art everywhere, from a painter's canvas in her father's studio to the expressive fashion on the streets of London or the beaches of Ibiza. These early years instilled in her not only a love of beauty but an understanding of its power to shape identity and experience. The lessons she absorbed in those formative years did not vanish as she grew older; they became the threads woven through the entirety of her future work.

Her story begins here, with a childhood framed by color, performance, and expression. The world of her upbringing gave her the tools to see beauty not as surface but as substance, not as ornament but as art. And while the chapters that followed would see her move from observer to participant, from experimenting child to trained artist, the roots of her journey lie firmly in the homes, streets, and studios of London and Ibiza, where a

Charlotte Tilbury biography

painter's daughter learned that artistry could shape the way people see themselves and the world.

Chapter 2: Entering the World of Beauty

Charlotte Tilbury's introduction to the world of beauty was not born in boardrooms or fashion studios but in the personal, tactile experience of discovering makeup as a form of expression. Growing up between London, where she was born, and Ibiza, where her family spent a significant portion of her childhood, she was surrounded by creative influences that encouraged experimentation. Her father, Lance Tilbury, was a painter, and the atmosphere of artistic freedom in Ibiza made color, texture, and transformation part of daily life. For Charlotte, cosmetics were never just about surface decoration. They became a language, a way to project confidence, and a tool for shaping how she felt about herself in different moments.

Her first real encounter with makeup as self-expression came in her teenage years. Living on the island of Ibiza during the 1980s exposed her to a culture that was open, expressive, and eclectic. The island was known for its free-spirited energy, drawing artists, musicians, and performers from across Europe. Charlotte observed how women—and men—used makeup not only to accentuate features but to craft entire identities. Lipstick could transform a mood, eyeliner could create mystery, and foundation could build a stage-ready version of the self. For someone with a keen eye for color and artistry, these early impressions resonated deeply. They planted the notion that beauty was not about conformity but about amplification and reinvention.

Charlotte has often recalled the transformative effect of her first experiences with mascara and eyeliner. They gave her a sense of power, altering how she presented herself to the world and how others responded to her. At an age when many young people struggle with self-confidence, she realized makeup could be both armor and an amplifier. That awareness stayed with her and became a central part of her future philosophy: makeup was not superficial but empowering, a medium that allowed people to feel like the best version of themselves.

By the time she reached her teenage years in London, her fascination with cosmetics had grown from curiosity to conviction. She was captivated by the visual impact makeup artists could create in magazines, music videos, and films. The 1980s were an era defined by bold makeup looks, from the electric colors of pop stars to the sculpted features seen in high fashion editorials. Charlotte immersed herself in these images, studying how eyeliner could change the shape of an eye or how contouring could redefine the architecture of a face. She began practicing on herself and her friends, experimenting with colors and techniques, and slowly building a confidence in her ability to transform ideas into looks.

The decision to pursue makeup artistry as a profession did not happen overnight, but by her late teens she was convinced that this was the path she wanted to take. She saw the artistry behind the work of professionals in the fashion industry and understood that makeup was a career as much as it was a passion. Her ambition led her to formal training, and in 1992 she enrolled at the Glauca Rossi School of Makeup in London. This choice marked the official beginning of her professional journey.

The Glauca Rossi School was already respected in the industry, known for its rigorous approach to teaching makeup artistry. For Charlotte, it provided not only technical skills but also an immersion in the discipline of the profession. The school emphasized precision, creativity, and an understanding of how makeup interacted with light, photography, and movement. These were essential skills for someone aiming to work in fashion and editorial contexts, where the smallest detail could determine whether a look succeeded or failed.

Charlotte threw herself into the training. She learned the foundations of makeup application, from skin preparation to color matching, and studied advanced techniques such as contouring, shading, and creating looks that would withstand the scrutiny of cameras. She also absorbed lessons in how to work under pressure, collaborate with photographers and stylists, and adapt quickly to different faces and environments. The school exposed her to the breadth of possibilities within the profession, from theatrical and stage makeup to the subtler artistry required in editorial shoots.

What stood out most during her time at Glauca Rossi was her ability to combine technical mastery with creativity. She was not content to simply replicate standard looks. Instead, she experimented, blending her early influences from Ibiza's expressive culture with the precision she was learning in class. Teachers and peers noticed her flair for bold choices, her eye for color, and her instinct for bringing out the best in a face. These qualities began to distinguish her, even at a stage when she was still a student learning the fundamentals.

Building confidence in artistry requires more than training; it demands real-world application. After graduating from Glauca Rossi, Charlotte began testing her skills on friends, acquaintances, and small assignments. These early steps were critical, allowing her to refine techniques in practical settings and develop the interpersonal skills that makeup artists need when working closely with clients. She understood that artistry was as much about making people feel at ease as it was about creating striking visuals. This combination of technical ability and personal connection became a hallmark of her style.

In the early 1990s, when Charlotte was establishing her foundation as an artist, London was a dynamic hub for fashion and culture. The city was experiencing a creative

Charlotte Tilbury biography

resurgence, with young designers, photographers, and musicians pushing boundaries. Charlotte's education placed her at the center of this energy, and her growing confidence allowed her to seize opportunities as they appeared. Every small job, every face she worked on, added to her experience and reinforced her belief that she was not just participating in beauty but shaping it.

Her confidence was not merely about skill but also about vision. She saw makeup as transformative, both for the wearer and for the broader culture of style and self-expression. This conviction was rooted in those first teenage encounters with cosmetics, strengthened by formal training at Glauca Rossi, and tested in the early years of her practice. It became the driving force behind her career, guiding her choices and giving her the assurance that she could stand out in a competitive industry.

By 1993, Charlotte Tilbury had completed her training and was actively working as a professional makeup artist. She was no longer the young girl experimenting with eyeliner in Ibiza or studying images in magazines; she was equipped with skills, experience, and a growing portfolio. Her education had given her the technical tools, and her personal background had given her the creative instincts. Together, they created a foundation strong enough to support the remarkable career that lay ahead.

In those first years after school, Charlotte was often described by those around her as ambitious, charismatic, and tireless. She possessed the rare combination of raw talent and relentless drive, a pairing that set her apart from many of her peers. Makeup was not just a job to her; it was a calling, and she approached every opportunity as a chance to prove that. Her confidence in artistry, carefully nurtured from her earliest experiments to her rigorous education, was no longer just a personal strength but a professional asset.

The phase of her life that began with teenage curiosity and culminated in the halls of the Glauca Rossi School marked a turning point. Charlotte Tilbury had entered the world of beauty not through chance but through conviction, guided by a belief in the transformative power of makeup and a determination to master her craft. She emerged from this period not only as a trained artist but as someone who understood that beauty could be a vehicle for self-expression, empowerment, and, eventually, influence on a global scale.

The story of Charlotte Tilbury's beginnings in beauty is, at its core, a testament to the power of passion combined with discipline. From those first encounters with cosmetics in Ibiza to the structured lessons of Glauca Rossi and the growing confidence she displayed in early assignments, every step reinforced her commitment to artistry. By the mid-1990s, she was poised to take the foundation she had built and apply it to an industry eager for new voices and fresh visions. What distinguished her was not only skill but the confidence to believe that she had something unique to offer. That belief, shaped during these formative years, would carry her into the next stages of her journey with momentum and clarity.

PART II: ESTABLISHING A MAKEUP CAREER

Charlotte Tilbury had laid the groundwork through education and early discovery, but training alone could not guarantee a place in the highly competitive world of beauty. The next phase of her journey was about stepping beyond classrooms and experiments into the fast-paced arenas of fashion shows, editorial shoots, and professional collaborations. Part II follows how she built her career in makeup artistry, proving her talent in real-world settings and establishing a reputation that would open doors to some of the most influential names in fashion and photography.

Charlotte Tilbury biography

Chapter 3: From London to the Fashion Runways

Charlotte Tilbury's career in the 1990s carried the raw energy of an industry that was reinventing itself at the close of one century and the beginning of another. London had always been one of fashion's great capitals, but in those years it became a particularly charged environment for new creativity. Young designers were beginning to push against traditional boundaries, photographers were introducing new visual languages, and supermodels were shaping a global culture around style. It was in this climate that Tilbury established herself as a working makeup artist, determined to prove that she had both the technical command and the imagination to belong on the most competitive runways and editorial sets of the decade.

Her path was not straightforward, nor was it handed to her. After completing her training at the Glauca Rossi School of Makeup in London in 1992, she faced the daunting task of building a freelance career from the ground up. The city was full of other talented artists vying for the same opportunities, and the fashion world had little patience for inexperience. Yet Tilbury was driven not only by skill but by a vision of what beauty could be. She wanted to redefine how makeup functioned in the storytelling of fashion, moving it beyond background detail and into a central, expressive role.

In those early freelance years, Tilbury accepted any assignment that could sharpen her abilities and place her work in front of influential eyes. She worked on test shoots with young photographers who, like her, were trying to make their names in London's restless creative scene. Some of those photographers would later become leading figures in fashion photography, and their early collaborations gave her an important foothold. She also immersed herself in runway work, where the backstage pace was frantic, the schedules unforgiving, and the standards exacting. The ability to deliver flawless looks under intense pressure was the currency that earned makeup artists future calls, and Tilbury was quick to adapt.

Charlotte Tilbury biography

Her work was defined by precision and an intuitive grasp of how makeup translated on different stages and under varying lights. On a runway, makeup needed to stand out from a distance and survive under blinding spotlights. On editorial shoots, the camera picked up subtleties, demanding softer gradations and a deeper understanding of texture and balance. Tilbury excelled in both contexts, which made her a versatile choice for stylists and photographers seeking someone who could align makeup with broader creative visions.

By 1994, Tilbury began working with photographers who were shaping new aesthetics in fashion. One of the most significant figures in her career was Mario Testino. His images combined glamour with an immediacy that defined much of fashion photography in the 1990s. Working with Testino provided Tilbury a platform to showcase makeup that could elevate a photograph's entire mood. Their collaboration would become a lasting partnership, but in those formative years, it gave her exposure to international magazines and campaigns that multiplied her visibility in the industry.

Charlotte Tilbury biography

Around the same time, Tilbury also worked with Mert Alas and Marcus Piggott, better known as Mert & Marcus. The duo, whose partnership began in the mid-1990s, quickly became known for bold, hyper-stylized imagery that demanded equally striking makeup. Tilbury's ability to sculpt faces that matched their cinematic vision cemented her as a trusted collaborator. With them, she contributed to a new visual language that emphasized drama, intensity, and surreal beauty. This kind of work helped distinguish her style as one that was neither timid nor conventional.

London's runways were an equally important arena for Tilbury. By 1996, she was backstage at shows that drew global attention, applying looks that had to be replicated across dozens of models under impossible time constraints. Designers wanted makeup that complemented but did not overshadow their collections, and Tilbury understood how to balance artistry with discipline. Her reputation grew as someone who could create cohesion across a show while still offering individuality to each model's face. These backstage experiences taught her not only speed and technical control but also leadership, as she increasingly directed small teams of assistants.

Collaboration with designers was critical to her rise. Alexander McQueen, whose shows in the 1990s were marked by theatricality and conceptual daring, offered a creative environment where Tilbury's imagination could thrive. His collections often demanded makeup that was as much a narrative tool as the garments themselves, and Tilbury's contribution was integral in bringing those visions to life. Working on McQueen's runway shows placed her at the forefront of fashion's avant-garde, proving her ability to handle the most experimental of briefs.

Her growing reputation also brought her into contact with major fashion houses beyond London. She began contributing to shows in Paris and Milan, where she adapted to different traditions and expectations. Each fashion capital had its own culture, and Tilbury's capacity to move between them showed her adaptability. Whether working on minimal, sleek aesthetics for Italian designers or bolder, more artistic statements in Paris, she showed an ability to align her artistry with varying brand identities.

Editorial work remained central throughout this period. Magazines such as *Vogue*, *Vanity Fair*, and *The Face* became platforms where her makeup could reach international audiences. Editorial shoots required a different discipline from runway work. They offered time to craft details, to experiment with textures, and to work closely with photographers in shaping the mood of an image. Tilbury's editorial contributions during the 1990s reflected her versatility. She could create ethereal natural looks, but she was equally adept at dramatic, high-glamour transformations. This range made her a favorite among editors and stylists seeking visual impact.

It was also during this decade that Tilbury began working with supermodels whose names defined the era. Kate Moss, Naomi Campbell, and Christy Turlington were among the faces she helped prepare for shoots and shows. Her work with Moss, in particular, was emblematic of the close creative relationships that can shape careers. Moss embodied a new kind of beauty in the 1990s, and Tilbury's makeup enhanced that image, reinforcing the cultural shift from polished perfection to a more natural, undone aesthetic.

The pace of freelance life was grueling. Tilbury often moved from one city to another in rapid succession, carrying her kit across airports and hotel rooms, always preparing for the next assignment. The demands of fashion weeks meant sleepless nights and constant deadlines, but she thrived in the intensity. Each show or shoot added another layer to her growing reputation, and her presence in both London and international fashion scenes became increasingly steady.

By 1997, Tilbury was no longer just one of many freelance artists hoping for recognition. She had carved out a distinctive place in the industry. Photographers, editors, and designers sought her out not only for technical expertise but for the creativity and energy she brought to projects. Her looks carried a signature quality: bold, glamorous, and transformative, yet always mindful of the overall vision. She was not imposing her style on the work but rather integrating her artistry into the fabric of fashion's changing language.

Charlotte Tilbury biography

This ability to align herself with larger creative movements while still standing out as an individual artist proved decisive. The late 1990s positioned her as one of the most in-demand makeup artists in Europe. Campaigns for luxury brands, editorial spreads in major magazines, and prominent runway assignments became part of her portfolio. Tilbury's name circulated within fashion circles as an artist who could be relied upon for both reliability and originality.

By 1999, the decade closed with Charlotte Tilbury firmly established on the fashion runways and within the editorial world. The years of relentless freelance work had paid off, bringing her into collaboration with some of the most influential figures in fashion. Her artistry had evolved from simple application to conceptual contribution, shaping the way makeup was integrated into photography and runway shows. She had proven that she could thrive in the most demanding environments and contribute to the creation of iconic fashion imagery.

Chapter 4: Collaborations with Photographers and Models

When Charlotte Tilbury began working in the 1990s, she quickly learned that the beauty industry was as much about collaboration as it was about individual artistry. Makeup artists could spend hours perfecting a look, but if the photographer's lens did not capture it, or if the model's energy did not bring it to life, the effect would fall flat. For Tilbury, partnerships with the right people became not only central to her creative output but essential to shaping her professional identity. Among these, her sustained collaborations with Mario Testino, Mert Alas, and Marcus Piggott, and a circle of models led by Kate Moss would prove pivotal. Through them, Tilbury found the stage on which to refine her ideas of glamour and create the visual language that became her signature.

Her path to working with Mario Testino was a turning point. Testino, born in Peru and established as one of the most sought-after fashion photographers of his generation, had risen to fame in the 1990s through his

Charlotte Tilbury biography

distinctive ability to capture intimacy and vibrancy in fashion images. When Tilbury began working with him in the same decade, she entered a creative partnership that extended for years and reached into the highest tiers of fashion. Testino's shoots for *Vogue*, *Vanity Fair*, and international advertising campaigns required makeup that not only flattered but defined the mood of the story being told. Tilbury excelled at this. She understood that Testino's photography thrived on warmth and immediacy, and she responded by creating looks that enhanced the skin's natural glow, emphasized bold lips when the mood required it, and always made the models appear both approachable and aspirational.

In the 1990s and 2000s, Tilbury worked on many of Testino's shoots that would later become iconic. His portfolio with Kate Moss, Gisele Bündchen, and other leading figures often bore Tilbury's imprint. Kate Moss, in particular, became a central figure in this circle of collaboration. Tilbury's artistry on Moss set new standards for what modern glamour looked like. Moving away from stiff, overly polished styles of the past, Tilbury leaned into a sultry, smudged eye, a glowing complexion, and lips that could shift from barely-there nude to bold red depending on the narrative. The now-classic "rock chic" look that came to be associated with Moss in the 1990s was not only her natural presence but also Tilbury's precise makeup vision.

Moss was already a cultural phenomenon, but Tilbury's work amplified her impact. Together with Testino, they created editorial images that reverberated through the fashion industry. Campaigns for houses like Gucci, Tom Ford, and Burberry carried Tilbury's artistic signature. It was not simply about applying eyeliner or selecting the right shade of foundation. Tilbury understood the alchemy of context. If Testino wanted to highlight Moss as carefree and luminous, Tilbury adjusted her palette to favor radiant skin, bronzed highlights, and soft, sensual eyes. If the shoot called for drama and edge, she emphasized stronger contrasts, deeper shades, and sharper contours. The flexibility and precision of her approach made her invaluable to Testino's team.

While Testino provided the traditional glamour lens of the 1990s, Tilbury's partnership with the duo Mert Alas and Marcus Piggott offered a new canvas for her creativity in the 2000s and 2010s. Known professionally as Mert & Marcus, the pair became some of the most influential fashion photographers of the early twenty-first century. Their style was unmistakable: hyper-real, digitally enhanced, drenched in bold color and sharp contrasts. Working with them required a different sensibility than with Testino, and Tilbury adapted seamlessly. She recognized that their high-saturation images demanded makeup that could withstand intense lighting and post-production editing without losing depth or dimension.

Tilbury rose to the challenge, crafting looks that complemented Mert & Marcus's futuristic aesthetic. Skin had to appear flawless yet alive. Eye makeup needed to be both graphic and fluid, bold enough to stand out in a heavily stylized image. Tilbury embraced metallics, high-shine finishes, and sculpted features. These collaborations pushed her to experiment with textures and tones that would later influence her product lines. The exaggerated yet polished aesthetic of Mert & Marcus's photographs aligned with Tilbury's love for drama, and together they produced editorials and campaigns that defined the visual identity of a new fashion era.

Among the models who brought these collaborations to life, Kate Moss remained central, but Tilbury also worked with a wider roster of icons, including Naomi Campbell, Gisele Bündchen, and Cara Delevingne. Each offered a unique presence, and Tilbury adapted her artistry accordingly. With Naomi Campbell, she highlighted strong bone structure and glowing skin, enhancing the natural radiance that made Campbell one of the world's most enduring supermodels. With Gisele Bündchen, she leaned into bronzed tones and fresh finishes that amplified Bündchen's athletic, sun-kissed appeal. Cara Delevingne's distinct eyebrows and rebellious edge offered yet another palette, where Tilbury balanced bold brows with playful lips and striking eyeliner.

It was through these collaborations that Tilbury honed what became her recognizable style of glamour. She blended old Hollywood influences with modern techniques, creating a look that was both timeless and current. Tilbury's glamour was never about masking or rigid perfection. It was about amplifying personality, heightening sensuality, and making images memorable. Her smoky eyes became legendary, her skin work admired for its luminosity, and her lip choices studied by fans and professionals alike.

Her work on campaigns and editorials with these photographers and models built a reputation that extended far beyond the industry. Audiences worldwide absorbed the imagery in glossy magazines, billboards, and advertisements. The consistency of Tilbury's artistry helped to cement the visual codes of the fashion world in the 1990s and 2000s. Women who admired Moss's effortless chic or Bündchen's radiant glow often sought to replicate the look, not always realizing that the unifying element behind these diverse images was Tilbury's hand.

The collaboration with Testino and Mert & Marcus also solidified Tilbury's role as a trusted artist among photographers who valued reliability under pressure. High-profile fashion shoots often required long hours, rapid adjustments, and the ability to translate broad creative concepts into precise visual outcomes. Tilbury's adaptability made her indispensable. Photographers could articulate a mood—sensuality, power, innocence—and Tilbury could translate it into color, texture, and contour. That ability to transform abstract ideas into tangible beauty became one of her greatest strengths.

Her growing circle of collaborators also ensured that her artistry reached global campaigns for major luxury houses. She became involved in advertising work for Dior, Louis Vuitton, and Tom Ford, among others. Each campaign added another layer to her portfolio and reinforced her presence at the highest levels of the fashion and beauty industries. These were not just jobs but opportunities to expand her aesthetic vocabulary. A Dior campaign might call for refinement and elegance, while Tom Ford emphasized bold sensuality. Tilbury adjusted to each seamlessly while retaining the unmistakable touch of her signature glamour.

The impact of these collaborations is visible in the way certain beauty tropes became standard. The bronzed, glowing complexion, once seen as seasonal, became a year-round staple. The sultry, smoky eye was no longer a look reserved for dramatic evenings but something women attempted to integrate into everyday life. These shifts were not simply the result of changing fashion but the influence of images Tilbury created with her collaborators. Her artistry filtered into mainstream beauty culture through repetition across covers, campaigns, and celebrity appearances.

By the time the 2010s arrived, Tilbury's status as one of the most influential makeup artists of her generation was secure. Her collaborations with Testino had given her global visibility, her work with Mert & Marcus kept her on the cutting edge, and her artistry on models like Kate Moss gave her looks a cultural permanence. Together, these collaborations provided the foundation for a recognizable style of glamour that became her signature. It was bold but never harsh, luminous but never artificial, seductive but never inaccessible.

The consistency of Tilbury's artistic vision across these partnerships did not come from rigid adherence to formulas but from an instinctive understanding of beauty as performance. She knew when to hold back and when to amplify, when a model's natural features should dominate and when drama should steal the scene. This balance made her work distinctive and enduring.

By shaping faces that would be immortalized in fashion's most circulated images, Tilbury built more than a résumé. She established a reputation as the artist behind the look of an era. Her collaborations with Testino, Mert & Marcus, and her close creative bonds with models like Kate Moss ensured that her artistry would not remain backstage but would stand as part of the cultural record of modern fashion.

These years laid down the DNA of Tilbury's glamour. The emphasis on glowing skin, the smoky eyes, and the balance of natural beauty and high drama—these became the visual codes that later defined her brand. Long before she put her name on packaging, her artistry had already become a brand in itself, recognizable across magazines, campaigns, and runways. The collaborations of this period were more than work assignments. They were the crucible in which Charlotte Tilbury forged the style that would one day captivate not just fashion insiders but millions of women around the world.

Chapter 5: British Vogue and Editorial Influence

When Charlotte Tilbury accepted the role of Beauty Editor-at-Large for *British Vogue* in 2003, she stepped into a platform that was not only prestigious but also historically influential in shaping ideas of fashion and beauty for millions of readers worldwide. For decades, *Vogue* had served as the cultural barometer of style, dictating the trends of each season, elevating new talents, and cementing the careers of designers, photographers, and models. For Tilbury, this appointment signified more than an editorial title; it was the recognition of her growing authority in the beauty industry and her ability to communicate artistry in a language that transcended backstage fashion shows.

By the time she joined *Vogue* in this capacity, Tilbury had already built a reputation in editorial circles as a makeup artist who could translate the essence of a designer's vision into beauty looks that resonated beyond the catwalk. Her tenure at *Vogue* allowed her to do something slightly different: it placed her in a position where she could shape not only the immediate aesthetics of fashion imagery but also the wider cultural conversation around beauty itself. In the 2000s, *British Vogue* was undergoing a period of renewal. The magazine was balancing tradition with modernity, seeking to retain its long-standing prestige while appealing to a younger, more global readership. Tilbury's presence fitted neatly into this evolution, as her artistry combined classic glamour with a contemporary sensibility that spoke to women seeking beauty both aspirational and attainable.

As Beauty Editor-at-Large, Tilbury was not tasked with writing monthly beauty columns or product roundups. Instead, her role was to contribute vision, ideas, and artistry that influenced the way beauty was presented within the magazine. This meant working directly with the editorial team, shaping photo shoots, and collaborating with photographers and models to produce spreads that captured attention. Her input extended to defining seasonal trends, offering creative insight, and bridging the gap between the backstage

Charlotte Tilbury biography

world she knew intimately and the glossy pages of one of fashion's most important publications.

Tilbury's first major contributions in 2003 came at a moment when the beauty industry was shifting its priorities. After the turn of the millennium, there was a growing emphasis on individuality and diversity of looks, moving away from a singular ideal of beauty. *British Vogue* was increasingly attentive to these shifts, and Tilbury's artistry, with its blend of theatricality and natural appeal, provided a means to showcase beauty as multifaceted. She championed looks that celebrated confidence and personality rather than rigid conformity, and her influence could be seen in covers and features where models wore makeup that enhanced rather than disguised their identities.

The role also elevated her visibility in the fashion press. While makeup artists had long been acknowledged within the industry, few were household names. Tilbury's position at *Vogue* amplified her profile beyond backstage whispers. She became someone whose name was printed in one of the world's most influential fashion magazines, reinforcing her credibility as both a creator

Charlotte Tilbury biography

and a commentator. The visibility offered by *Vogue* positioned her as a trusted authority, not just for industry insiders but for the wider public who looked to the magazine for guidance on how to understand and adopt new trends.

Throughout the 2000s, Tilbury collaborated on numerous shoots that bore the unmistakable mark of her artistry. Working with photographers such as Mario Testino, Craig McDean, and Mert & Marcus, she helped craft images that were not only visually striking but also carried a specific attitude. Tilbury's makeup often lent these images an air of boldness and strength, qualities that became associated with her signature style. Whether it was the smoky eye that became one of her trademarks or the luminous skin finish that gave models an otherworldly glow, her hand in *Vogue* shoots pushed beauty presentation toward a modern glamour that appealed to a generation newly immersed in celebrity culture and red-carpet aesthetics.

In many ways, her role at *Vogue* allowed her to test ideas that would later become central to her entrepreneurial endeavors. She experimented with looks that were both editorially dramatic and consumer-friendly. Features in *Vogue* often presented makeup as an accessible form of empowerment, with Tilbury's artistry demonstrating how a sweep of eyeliner or the right shade of lipstick could transform more than an appearance—it could transform mood and presence. This philosophy resonated strongly with readers who sought beauty not merely as ornamentation but as a tool for confidence.

The 2000s also marked a period of heightened competition among fashion magazines, with *Vogue* seeking to assert its dominance against newer rivals and digital platforms that were beginning to gain traction. In this landscape, Tilbury's contributions became increasingly valuable. Her ability to deliver looks that captured attention in print and also translated to real-life adoption gave *Vogue* a unique edge. She understood that the modern reader did not only want aspirational beauty imagery but also practical inspiration they could incorporate into their own routines. Tilbury's work managed to bridge this divide, making editorial beauty aspirational without being unattainable.

Charlotte Tilbury biography

Her influence in *Vogue* extended beyond the pages themselves. The association with the magazine granted her access to a network of editors, stylists, and cultural figures that expanded her professional visibility. She attended industry events under the banner of *Vogue*, further strengthening her profile in the eyes of designers and celebrities alike. This network would prove instrumental in reinforcing her reputation as one of the most in-demand makeup artists of her generation.

Charlotte Tilbury's tenure as Beauty Editor-at-Large coincided with the rise of celebrity culture in the 2000s, when the lines between fashion magazines, red-carpet coverage, and entertainment media began to blur. *British Vogue* was deeply entwined in this cultural moment, frequently featuring celebrities alongside models on its covers and in its pages. Tilbury's artistry played a role in shaping how these celebrities were presented, providing looks that merged high fashion with mass appeal. By working on shoots that featured some of the world's most recognizable faces, she expanded her influence further, as readers and fans sought to emulate the looks they admired in the pages of *Vogue*.

Charlotte Tilbury biography

The magazine also allowed her to voice opinions on the direction of beauty. Through features and interviews, Tilbury was able to articulate her philosophy on makeup as a force for empowerment. She often spoke about the transformative power of makeup, how it could boost self-confidence, and how it should be seen as a tool of expression rather than a mask. These perspectives were not only quoted in the pages of *Vogue* but also echoed throughout other press outlets, creating a ripple effect that reinforced her standing as a thought leader in the beauty space.

One of the striking aspects of her period with *Vogue* was the consistency of her influence throughout the decade. Even as fashion trends evolved, Tilbury maintained a voice that was relevant and contemporary. She adapted her artistry to suit shifting styles—from minimalist aesthetics that dominated some seasons to the more maximalist glamour that returned in others—while always maintaining her signature sense of drama and allure. This adaptability was key to her staying power within *Vogue*, as it ensured her work remained aligned with the magazine's ever-evolving creative direction.

Charlotte Tilbury biography

By the time the decade closed, Charlotte Tilbury's name had become inseparable from editorial beauty in Britain. Her position at *Vogue* had not only elevated her profile but had also allowed her to refine a narrative around beauty that combined artistry, empowerment, and glamour. She was no longer just a backstage force known to fashion insiders; she had become a visible figure in the broader cultural landscape of beauty. Her editor-at-large role provided her with both credibility and a platform to broadcast her vision, a combination that secured her position as one of the defining voices in 21st-century beauty culture.

Looking back at her years with *British Vogue*, it is clear that this chapter of her career represented a turning point. The magazine gave her the authority of a platform that influenced millions and provided her with opportunities to shape trends, define imagery, and expand her visibility far beyond the confines of the runway or studio. Her artistry reached audiences who might never attend a fashion show but who religiously followed the pages of *Vogue* for guidance on how to understand beauty in their own lives.

Charlotte Tilbury biography

Her contributions to *British Vogue* in the 2000s helped redefine how makeup was positioned within the fashion press. It was no longer a secondary element supporting clothing but an integral part of the overall aesthetic narrative. Through her work, Charlotte Tilbury emphasized that beauty was central to the story of style, deserving of the same attention as garments, accessories, and photography. This integration of makeup into the heart of fashion storytelling was a legacy of her editorial influence, one that resonated through the industry and continues to shape how beauty is presented in fashion publications today.

For Tilbury personally, these years established her as more than a makeup artist. They positioned her as a cultural authority whose vision reached across different audiences, cementing her reputation as someone who not only created beauty but also defined its meaning within the pages of one of the world's most respected magazines. Her role at *Vogue* was not just a professional accolade; it was a platform that validated her influence and broadcast it globally, laying a foundation for the next stages of her career.

Charlotte Tilbury biography

PART III: BECOMING A PUBLIC BEAUTY AUTHORITY

Charlotte Tilbury's influence was no longer confined to the pages of magazines or the runways of fashion weeks. As her artistry reached wider audiences, she began to emerge as a public figure in her own right, trusted not only by designers and editors but by women across the world seeking inspiration. This part traces how she stepped into the spotlight, built a recognizable voice in beauty, and transformed from a backstage artist into a visible authority whose presence reshaped the way beauty was perceived and celebrated.

Chapter 6: Breakthrough as a Celebrity Makeup Artist

Charlotte Tilbury's transition from a respected figure in editorial fashion to a globally recognized celebrity makeup artist marked a decisive turning point in her career. Until the late 1990s, she was already establishing her place backstage at fashion weeks and within the pages of magazines, but the move into the world of celebrities and red-carpet appearances gave her artistry an entirely new platform. Makeup was no longer confined to the studio lights of high-fashion photography or the controlled chaos of runway shows. Instead, it became a visible statement broadcast across television screens, newspapers, and later digital platforms that fed an ever-growing appetite for celebrity culture. This period would propel Tilbury into a new kind of visibility, linking her name with some of the most famous faces of film, fashion, and music.

The red carpet quickly became a proving ground. For an artist whose craft had largely been appreciated within the fashion community, Hollywood premieres and award shows offered an audience that stretched far beyond the industry. These events demanded a different kind of artistry. Under the glare of cameras, every detail mattered: the precision of eyeliner, the texture of skin, and the exact shade of lipstick that could transform a look from conventional to unforgettable. Tilbury excelled at this level of pressure, demonstrating a combination of technical mastery and intuition that allowed her to anticipate how makeup would translate under flash photography and moving cameras.

Her work with Kate Moss was among the first celebrity associations that drew wider attention. Moss, already one of the world's most photographed women, often carried the kind of sultry, rock-and-roll glamour that became synonymous with Tilbury's style. Their collaborations were not restricted to editorials but extended to public appearances where Moss's looks defined headlines. The balance of smoky eyes, nude lips, and luminous skin became part of a recognizable aesthetic that critics and fans alike associated with Tilbury. The consistency with which Moss appeared flawless in settings ranging from Cannes premieres to

Charlotte Tilbury biography

London fashion events positioned Tilbury as an indispensable figure behind the star.

At the same time, Tilbury's work expanded into Hollywood circles. She began collaborating with actresses whose careers demanded a level of red-carpet perfection that would capture the world's attention. Penélope Cruz became one of her high-profile clients, and their collaboration brought together the allure of Spanish elegance with Tilbury's artistry. Cruz's appearances at international film festivals, particularly Cannes, showcased makeup looks that emphasized smoldering eyes and glowing skin, translating Tilbury's fashion-informed techniques into cinematic moments. These looks not only elevated Cruz's style but also reinforced Tilbury's reputation as the artist who could create timeless glamour with a modern edge.

Tilbury also developed a creative bond with Amal Clooney, whose emergence as a global figure brought with it a new kind of red-carpet sophistication. When Clooney appeared at events alongside George Clooney, her presence carried both political and cultural weight. Tilbury's makeup ensured that her client's elegance never faltered under the global spotlight. The subtle yet striking looks she crafted for Clooney demonstrated her adaptability, capable of complementing couture gowns without overwhelming them. This balance of refinement and allure became one of Tilbury's hallmarks and reinforced her place as the choice of women who wanted to command attention without sacrificing authenticity.

Her clientele was not limited to actresses. Tilbury's artistry resonated strongly in the music industry, where performers required looks that could survive stage lights, cameras, and an audience expecting spectacle. She collaborated with Jennifer Lopez, helping to refine the singer's already-iconic image with makeup that accentuated Lopez's glowing skin and bold features. Lopez's appearances at award shows and performances were frequently accompanied by commentary on her radiant beauty, with Tilbury's techniques playing a central role in defining that perception.

Rihanna also became a notable figure who worked with Tilbury during this era. As Rihanna's career gained momentum, her style choices placed her firmly in the category of cultural trendsetter. Tilbury's contribution to her red-carpet appearances showcased an ability to create daring, experimental looks without sacrificing polish. From bold lips to sharp eyeliner, the makeup spoke to Rihanna's fearless persona and connected Tilbury's artistry to a younger, more experimental audience.

Tilbury's expansion into the American entertainment scene also saw her working with actresses such as Nicole Kidman and Gwyneth Paltrow, each representing a different facet of Hollywood glamour. Kidman's porcelain complexion and refined presence allowed Tilbury to demonstrate her skill in creating ethereal, luminous skin that photographed beautifully under bright lights. Paltrow's appearances often leaned toward understated elegance, giving Tilbury space to showcase restraint and subtlety, proving that her artistry was not confined to bold statements but also excelled in quiet sophistication.

As these collaborations multiplied, so did Tilbury's presence on the world's most-watched stages. The Academy Awards, the Golden Globes, and international film festivals became recurring platforms for her work. Each appearance by her clients translated into headlines and photographs shared worldwide. At a time when celebrity culture was rapidly globalizing, Tilbury's makeup artistry was being consumed not only by those in attendance but by millions of people across print media, television broadcasts, and the growing influence of digital outlets.

The early 2000s were also significant for the way Tilbury began to define looks that were instantly recognizable as hers. Smoky eyes became a trademark, not in the heavy, smudged sense of the past, but in a way that balanced intensity with refinement. Her approach to contouring and highlighting brought dimension to faces without appearing artificial, long before these techniques became mainstream in beauty culture. Tilbury's ability to blend artistry with a sense of timeless glamour meant her work stood out even when trends shifted.

One of the defining elements of her breakthrough was how seamlessly she adapted her fashion background to the needs of celebrities. Fashion shoots often required drama, exaggeration, and experimental aesthetics. Red carpets, by contrast, demanded an artistry that could translate under scrutiny from every angle, withstand long hours of wear, and yet still capture individuality. Tilbury mastered this balance. She had an intuitive grasp of the relationship between makeup, lighting, and fabric, ensuring that her clients appeared cohesive from head to toe.

As her reputation spread, Tilbury began to receive formal recognition within the industry. She was regularly cited in beauty features by leading magazines, not only as the artist behind celebrity transformations but as a tastemaker influencing global beauty standards. By the late 2000s, her presence at red-carpet events was so consistent that her name was often mentioned alongside the designers whose gowns dominated the headlines. Makeup had become part of the larger narrative of celebrity style, and Tilbury had positioned herself as one of the key architects of that narrative.

Her collaborations with music stars extended beyond Lopez and Rihanna, including work with Taylor Swift and Selena Gomez at pivotal moments in their careers. These appearances often became part of defining eras for the artists, where a single look captured in photographs came to symbolize an album cycle or a cultural moment.

Charlotte Tilbury biography

Tilbury's artistry ensured that the makeup elevated rather than overshadowed, reinforcing her ability to enhance identity rather than impose it.

The growing list of high-profile clients not only solidified her reputation but also positioned her as a bridge between fashion, film, and music. Few makeup artists could move so fluidly between these worlds, understanding the unique demands of each while maintaining a consistent standard of excellence. This versatility became one of the most important aspects of her breakthrough.

By 2010, Charlotte Tilbury's status as a celebrity makeup artist was no longer in question. She had built a portfolio that spanned continents, industries, and cultural genres, making her name synonymous with glamour at the highest level. What distinguished her was not simply technical brilliance but her ability to infuse her work with personality. Every client looked like the best version of themselves, not a replica of someone else. This philosophy resonated in an industry that often struggled to balance authenticity with spectacle.

Charlotte Tilbury biography

The red carpet had given Tilbury something editorial work alone could not: visibility beyond the fashion elite. Her artistry was now a matter of public record, cataloged in images and televised broadcasts that reached audiences across the globe. The faces she painted became cultural reference points, the looks she created setting trends that rippled out into mainstream beauty culture. This was the moment when Charlotte Tilbury was no longer just a makeup artist working behind the scenes. She had become a name in her own right, one whose artistry carried the weight of influence at the highest levels of global celebrity.

This breakthrough period defined the trajectory of her career for years to come. By proving her ability to command red-carpet presence, she secured her place as the trusted hand behind some of the world's most visible women. The distinctiveness of her looks, the consistency of her results, and her ability to collaborate with stars across industries made her indispensable. The chapter of her life that began in fashion photography had evolved into something larger: the artistry of creating icons in the public eye.

Charlotte Tilbury biography

Charlotte Tilbury's red-carpet breakthrough was not an accident of timing or chance encounters. It was the product of years of honing skills, understanding faces, and learning how beauty could be both personal and global at once. With each brushstroke on celebrities who walked into the glare of cameras, she was not only elevating her clients but also establishing a signature presence that would follow her into the next, even more ambitious stages of her career.

Chapter 7: Industry Recognition and Awards

By the time Charlotte Tilbury had firmly established herself as one of the most in-demand makeup artists in the United Kingdom, her career entered a new phase defined not just by artistry but by recognition from the wider beauty and fashion establishment. Awards, honors, and institutional acknowledgements began to shape her public profile, elevating her beyond the backstage role of a trusted expert and into the broader arena where fashion councils, media platforms, and cultural institutions celebrated her contributions. This period was pivotal because it marked the moment when Tilbury was no longer regarded only as a creative technician but as a cultural figure whose work had changed the way beauty was perceived within fashion and popular culture.

Becoming a respected figure in the British beauty scene was never something that happened overnight. It required years of consistent innovation, collaboration with leading designers, photographers, and stylists, and an ability to keep her work relevant to shifting cultural tastes. By the late 2000s, Tilbury's name had become synonymous with the polished yet sultry aesthetic that dominated the covers of British fashion magazines. In the British beauty scene, respect is earned not just by talent but also by visibility, longevity, and influence. Tilbury had by this point amassed a reputation that checked all three boxes.

Her growing prominence was mirrored in the acknowledgement she received from British fashion councils and institutions that have long played the role of gatekeepers in determining which voices truly shape the industry. One of the most significant nods came from the British Fashion Council (BFC), which had always been central in elevating designers and creative figures who shaped the image of British fashion globally. Tilbury's regular collaborations with designers at London Fashion Week had already put her in close contact with the council's network, but her recognition went beyond seasonal work. The council increasingly saw her as a representative of British beauty's global influence, an artist who understood how makeup trends contributed to the storytelling of fashion as a whole.

Charlotte Tilbury biography

It is telling that in 2014, the same year her own brand debuted, the British Fashion Council named Charlotte Tilbury the winner of the Makeup Artist of the Year award at the Fashion Awards. This was a moment of immense significance. By this time, Tilbury was already highly respected among editors, photographers, and models, but the Fashion Awards carried a particular cultural weight in Britain. It was an acknowledgment not just of her artistry but of the way she had shaped contemporary beauty ideals across both editorial and commercial platforms. Receiving that award placed her alongside the most influential figures in the British fashion ecosystem, a community where recognition by peers has long been the measure of true influence.

The significance of that award went far beyond the personal trophy. It formalized what the fashion industry had known for years: Tilbury was not only a leading makeup artist but also an innovator. The award cemented her place in the canon of British creatives who had changed how the industry operated. It was a moment when her career narrative was not just about her individual achievements backstage but also about her contribution to the broader cultural landscape.

Her recognition did not stop there. The following years saw her profile expand through consistent acknowledgment at industry ceremonies. In 2015, Tilbury was honored at the Rodial Beautiful Awards with the Makeup Artist of the Year title, reinforcing her status as a professional at the very top of her field. This event, designed to celebrate those who embodied beauty and style in a modern sense, underscored Tilbury's role as a cultural figure whose artistry shaped how beauty was defined in Britain at the time.

By 2016, when she received the CEW (Cosmetic Executive Women) Achiever Award, Tilbury had proven that her influence went beyond artistry into leadership. CEW, a nonprofit organization dedicated to advancing women in the beauty industry, recognized Tilbury for her entrepreneurial and creative accomplishments. This award was especially meaningful because it placed her in the context of business leadership as well as creative artistry. She was recognized not simply as someone who transformed faces for runway shows but as a woman who was reshaping the future of beauty through innovation, inspiration, and ambition.

Acknowledgements like these reinforced Tilbury's role as a figure who bridged multiple aspects of the beauty landscape: artistry, entrepreneurship, cultural impact, and female empowerment. They also highlighted how unusual her career trajectory was. Makeup artists are often celebrated within small professional circles but rarely reach a level where institutional bodies view them as transformative figures worthy of national and international recognition. Tilbury broke that mold.

Her recognition also reflected how she became increasingly visible in mainstream media. Tilbury was not only celebrated at closed industry gatherings but also regularly appeared on television and in interviews, where her insights about beauty trends reached a much broader audience. She became a familiar presence on shows like "Good Morning Britain" and international programs where she discussed beauty as a tool of confidence and empowerment. These appearances helped shape her public image as not only an artist but also a communicator who could bring her expertise directly into the homes of everyday people.

In interviews with publications ranging from *Vogue* to *The Guardian*, Tilbury often articulated the philosophy behind her artistry in ways that resonated with both fashion insiders and general audiences. She emphasized that beauty was not just about superficial transformation but about confidence, personality, and empowerment. This articulation of a vision elevated her media profile, ensuring that recognition by councils and institutions was mirrored by a growing appreciation among the public.

One of the defining hallmarks of this period in her career was the British government's recognition of her contributions. In 2018, Tilbury was appointed Member of the Order of the British Empire (MBE) in the Queen's Birthday Honours for services to the beauty and cosmetics industry. This was not only a personal honor but also a milestone for the entire beauty profession. Makeup artists are seldom acknowledged at this level, and Tilbury's recognition underscored how she had transcended her role to become a cultural ambassador for

British creativity. The investiture ceremony at Buckingham Palace that year represented the formal acknowledgment of her work by the highest institutional body in the nation.

The MBE had implications beyond personal achievement. It signaled that the beauty industry, often dismissed as superficial or secondary compared to fashion or art, was being recognized for its cultural and economic importance. Tilbury's award was not just about her personal success but also about elevating beauty as an integral part of the British creative industries. This recognition placed her in the company of leading designers, musicians, and artists whose work had defined Britain's cultural output.

By the early 2020s, Tilbury's recognition was reflected in international awards as well. In 2020, she received the Isabella Blow Award for Fashion Creator at The Fashion Awards, one of the most prestigious honors in the industry. Named after the legendary British fashion editor and talent scout Isabella Blow, this award celebrates creative figures who have made an outstanding contribution to the fashion world. Tilbury's

Charlotte Tilbury biography

win underscored how her artistry and influence had become central to defining contemporary fashion imagery. The award was particularly poignant because Isabella Blow herself had been an early champion of creative talent in Britain, and Tilbury's recognition carried the weight of being seen as a transformative figure in that tradition.

This stream of recognition was not limited to awards ceremonies. Tilbury became a regular presence on magazine covers and features, not just as the artist behind the looks but as a subject in her own right. Publications like *Vogue*, *Harper's Bazaar*, and *The Times* profiled her achievements, emphasizing how she had turned artistry into influence. This visibility reinforced the perception that she was no longer behind the curtain but standing at the forefront as one of Britain's most recognizable creative entrepreneurs.

Television appearances further extended her reach. Tilbury was frequently invited to speak about her work, her philosophy, and her brand on both British and international platforms. Her ability to explain beauty in accessible terms, while still maintaining the glamour and charisma associated with her persona, made her a compelling media figure. Whether demonstrating products on screen or offering her insights into red carpet trends, she embodied a modern figure of expertise who could seamlessly transition between professional artistry and public influence.

By 2025, the cumulative effect of decades of awards, honors, and media appearances positioned Charlotte Tilbury as more than an artist or brand founder. She stood as a respected British creative leader whose career was punctuated by consistent acknowledgement from institutions that mattered. Every award carried significance not only for her personal narrative but also for what it said about the changing status of beauty within culture.

In charting these moments, it becomes clear that recognition was not incidental to Tilbury's career but an essential part of it. Each award, from the British Fashion Council's Makeup Artist of the Year in 2014 to the Isabella Blow Award in 2020 and the MBE in 2018, marked a milestone that showed how her influence had extended far beyond the makeup chair. Her visibility in

Charlotte Tilbury biography

media amplified that recognition, ensuring that her artistry was not confined to industry circles but celebrated by a much wider public.

The accumulation of honors and acknowledgements demonstrates how Charlotte Tilbury redefined what it means to be a makeup artist in Britain. She proved that artistry could command respect, that beauty could be treated with the seriousness afforded to fashion and art, and that an individual could rise from backstage to become a cultural figure recognized by councils, institutions, governments, and media alike. By 2025, she stood as a living example of how creative vision, when matched with consistency and ambition, could not only earn professional respect but also secure a lasting place in the cultural history of British beauty.

Chapter 8: From Makeup Chair to Global Stage

When Charlotte Tilbury first began to move from the anonymity of backstage artistry to the glare of public life, the shift was not accidental. It was carefully built upon years of credibility within fashion and beauty circles, but it also reflected her awareness that the industry was changing. The makeup artist was no longer simply a figure hidden behind the curtain at fashion weeks or on magazine shoots. By the 2000s, beauty professionals had begun to step forward as public personalities in their own right, and Tilbury recognized that visibility could amplify her influence and elevate her voice. This chapter follows how she made that transition, not only through her appearances and interviews but through the cultivation of a persona that was approachable, authoritative, and compelling to both industry peers and the public.

Charlotte's rise as a public figure unfolded in stages. In the 1990s she was primarily known within fashion and celebrity circles, working alongside models and photographers. By 2002, her role as Beauty Editor-at-Large for British Vogue gave her a platform to speak directly to audiences who consumed beauty trends in print. This was an early step in placing her name and voice outside of private workspaces. Yet her more visible transition occurred a decade later when her media appearances multiplied and her personality, already magnetic to those around her, became part of the story of her artistry.

One of the defining qualities that made her appearances resonate was her ability to speak about beauty in a way that felt inclusive. Makeup, long presented in fashion magazines as aspirational and often unattainable, became through her language a tool of empowerment and confidence. She presented herself not only as an expert but as a guide who wanted to share secrets that could help anyone, regardless of their level of experience. This style of communication positioned her differently from some contemporaries who maintained a distance between professional artistry and public accessibility.

Charlotte Tilbury biography

Television played a crucial role in establishing Tilbury's wider credibility. Appearances on programs such as Britain's *This Morning* allowed her to demonstrate techniques and speak about beauty trends in a way that made her work relatable to a mainstream audience. These were not niche industry interviews. They placed her in the living rooms of people who might never attend fashion weeks or read luxury magazines but were interested in the practical and aspirational elements of beauty. In doing so, Tilbury widened her reach and solidified the perception that she was more than a backstage figure.

By 2011 and 2012, her presence at high-profile events further strengthened this public-facing role. She became a visible figure at award ceremonies, fashion galas, and global brand events, not only working behind the scenes but appearing as a celebrated guest in her own right. Her distinctive look—glamorous red hair, smoky eye makeup, and a warm smile—became recognizable and tied to her emerging brand identity. Importantly, these appearances reinforced her authority. When she spoke about beauty, it was not simply as a professional but as a personality whose image embodied the glamour she was known for creating.

What set Tilbury apart in this new visibility was her balance of authority with approachability. She never spoke in a way that felt inaccessible or overly technical. Instead, she explained artistry with enthusiasm, peppering her speech with phrases that conveyed excitement and energy. She spoke about beauty as transformation, as a way to unlock confidence, and she did so in terms that were easy to follow. Her passion translated into authenticity, a trait that audiences instinctively recognized. This accessibility became a cornerstone of her persona, helping her establish a reputation as someone who was not only talented but generous with her expertise.

In 2013, when she launched her YouTube channel and began publishing tutorials, the move marked another leap into the global spotlight. For the first time, she was not only appearing on television or in interviews arranged by editors and producers. She was speaking directly to audiences around the world, controlling the narrative of her artistry. The tutorials were polished but infused with her personality. She laughed easily, she encouraged viewers with warmth, and she emphasized that anyone could achieve the looks she demonstrated. These videos built a digital community around her, extending her authority beyond professional circles into households worldwide.

Her approach worked. By 2014 and 2015, her tutorials had reached millions of views, and her presence online attracted an audience spanning demographics and geographies. This ability to speak directly to consumers rather than only through industry gatekeepers was crucial. It positioned her at the intersection of expertise and celebrity, creating a sense of intimacy between her and those who watched her videos. For many, Charlotte was no longer just a name associated with models or magazine credits. She became a personality they felt they knew.

Her appearances at fashion events also reflected this dual role. At the Cannes Film Festival in 2016, for example, she was seen not only working with celebrities but also giving interviews about beauty and red carpet trends. These opportunities reinforced the sense that her opinion mattered as much as her artistry. Journalists quoted her insights, and the industry treated her perspective as that of a leading authority. She was no longer framed as someone simply working behind the scenes but as an expert shaping the conversation around glamour and style.

As her reputation grew, Tilbury continued to cultivate this balance between expert and friend. She spoke with the authority of someone who had painted the faces of world-famous celebrities and styled countless magazine covers. Yet she paired that authority with stories from her own life, recalling the ways makeup empowered her personally and professionally. This combination of personal anecdote and professional expertise created a unique voice. It was authoritative but never intimidating, glamorous but never unrelatable.

The importance of her public persona extended beyond media appearances. It was integral to the way she presented her brand after its launch in 2013. She appeared in promotional campaigns herself, often demonstrating products on camera. She was not simply a founder who stayed behind the curtain while spokesmodels represented the brand. She became the face of her products, speaking directly to consumers, inviting them into her world, and guiding them step by step. This decision tied her identity inseparably to her company. The public associated Charlotte Tilbury not only with artistry but with an approachable figure who stood behind every product bearing her name.

By 2018, when she received an MBE for services to the beauty and cosmetics industry, her credibility had extended far beyond fashion circles. The award represented national recognition, affirming that her contributions were significant to British culture and commerce. The honor also reinforced her reputation as someone who could balance artistry with public authority. For audiences who followed her appearances, the recognition validated what they had already observed: she had become a figure whose influence stretched from private studios to global stages.

What made Tilbury's transition particularly effective was the timing. Her rise as a public persona coincided with a period when social media and digital content were transforming beauty. The public was becoming increasingly interested in hearing directly from experts and personalities, and she positioned herself exactly in that space. She did not wait for consumers to discover her through traditional channels. Instead, she embraced every opportunity to meet audiences where they were, whether in print, on television, or online. This adaptability ensured that her voice carried across platforms and generations.

Her reputation as an approachable yet authoritative figure has remained consistent into the 2020s. In interviews, she continues to speak with warmth and excitement, often highlighting how makeup can empower women to feel stronger, more confident, and more beautiful. She emphasizes both technical skill and emotional connection, ensuring that her audience sees her not only as an expert but as someone who genuinely cares about their experiences with beauty. This dual reputation has allowed her to maintain relevance even as trends and technologies evolve.

What emerges from examining her journey from the makeup chair to the global stage is a story of intentional visibility. Tilbury did not abandon her artistry; she expanded it. She realized that credibility could be amplified through presence, and she shaped that presence with precision. Her public appearances built recognition, her approachable language invited connection, and her authoritative expertise cemented trust. Together, these elements constructed a persona that was greater than the sum of its parts.

By 2025, Charlotte Tilbury stands not only as the founder of a global brand but as one of the most recognizable personalities in beauty. Her presence is as much a part of her legacy as her artistry. From television segments to digital tutorials, from red carpet interviews to national honors, she has crafted a public role that reinforces her expertise while making her approachable to millions. It is this balance that secured her credibility outside of backstage fashion and established her as a modern visionary whose influence resonates far beyond the makeup chair.

Charlotte Tilbury biography

PART IV: BUILDING CHARLOTTE TILBURY BEAUTY

The turning point in Charlotte Tilbury's career came when she stepped beyond the role of makeup artist and put her name on a brand that would redefine modern beauty. What began as artistry at the hands of one individual evolved into a global enterprise that merged creativity, luxury, and strategy. This part traces the foundation and growth of *Charlotte Tilbury Beauty*, showing how a personal vision was transformed into an international powerhouse with products, campaigns, and a brand identity that reshaped the beauty landscape.

Chapter 9: Founding the Brand in 2013

When Charlotte Tilbury launched her own makeup line in 2013, it was not a sudden leap into the unknown but the culmination of years of observing, testing, and understanding how women interacted with beauty. By that point, she had already spent decades behind the scenes of fashion shows, magazine shoots, and red-carpet events. Her brushes had painted the faces of some of the world's most recognizable models, actresses, and performers, but even as her reputation grew, she had begun to notice a persistent gap between the products available on the market and what both professionals and everyday consumers actually needed. The founding of Charlotte Tilbury Beauty was born from this recognition.

Luxury cosmetics in the early 2010s had prestige and glamour, but they often lacked accessibility. Many brands leaned heavily into exclusivity, creating products that were aspirational but intimidating. Makeup counters in department stores carried elegant packaging and high prices, but the marketing often left ordinary consumers unsure of what to choose or how to apply it. Charlotte

Charlotte Tilbury biography

Tilbury understood that glamour should not be an enigma. She had seen, through years of firsthand work, that the barrier for many women was not desire but confidence and guidance. She envisioned a brand that married the sophistication of luxury cosmetics with a voice that spoke directly to the consumer, teaching, inspiring, and empowering them in ways the traditional beauty world had not.

By 2011, Charlotte had already been laying the groundwork for her own line. She had built trust with audiences by sharing her artistry publicly through online tutorials and appearances, which distinguished her from the more mysterious image of many makeup artists at the time. While most professionals guarded their techniques closely, she took a different path, showing step-by-step how to create her signature looks. This transparency earned her a loyal following and proved that there was a large audience eager to learn from someone who not only had backstage authority but also the ability to communicate directly with consumers.

In 2012, she began working intensively on product development. She drew upon her years of experience using countless formulas from existing brands, taking note of their shortcomings and advantages. One of the products she insisted on perfecting was her Magic Cream, a rich moisturizer she had been mixing and applying on models for years during fashion weeks. It had become legendary among those who worked with her, restoring tired skin before shows and helping makeup glide on effortlessly. Bringing that once-personal backstage secret to the retail market would become one of her signature moves, exemplifying her ability to transform professional solutions into consumer must-haves.

On 2 September 2013, Charlotte Tilbury Beauty officially launched at Selfridges in London. The choice of Selfridges was significant. The store had long been a symbol of innovation in retail, known for blending luxury with accessibility and for being at the cutting edge of fashion and beauty presentations. Launching in such a prestigious setting sent a clear signal that Tilbury's brand was not only meant for professionals but designed to resonate with everyday women looking for transformative beauty products.

Charlotte Tilbury biography

The launch was orchestrated with careful attention to detail. Charlotte herself was at the center, greeting customers, explaining products, and embodying the glamorous, confident persona that had already made her a recognizable figure in the industry. The brand's distinctive packaging immediately stood out. With its deep, metallic burgundy tones and art deco accents, it was unmistakable on the shelves, reinforcing the sense of luxury while also carrying a warmth that felt approachable. Each product had a story, and Charlotte positioned them not as isolated items but as part of a larger beauty wardrobe.

The structure of the collection was innovative. Rather than simply releasing individual products, Charlotte introduced curated looks. There were ten signature looks, each with a name and personality, such as The Rebel, The Ingenue, and The Vintage Vamp. These looks provided consumers with a complete set of products to achieve a particular style, eliminating the uncertainty of choosing colors and combinations on their own. It was a format that gave women the reassurance of a makeup artist's guidance but in a form they could apply at home.

Charlotte Tilbury biography

For many, this was the bridge they needed to feel confident purchasing luxury makeup.

Consumer reception was immediate and intense. Lines formed at Selfridges as women and makeup enthusiasts gathered to see the new brand firsthand. Many were already familiar with Charlotte from her media presence and her reputation as a trusted artist. Now, they had access to her artistry in tangible form. Products like the Magic Cream sold quickly, and her lipsticks became an instant draw. The press coverage was extensive, with British newspapers, fashion magazines, and beauty editors highlighting the launch as a significant moment in the industry. The attention was not limited to the UK. International beauty media noted the arrival of a new force in luxury cosmetics, pointing out Charlotte's distinctive mix of artistry and showmanship.

The success of the launch was not accidental. Charlotte had crafted every aspect of her brand identity with intention. From the product formulas to the packaging design, from the naming of shades to the layout of counters, she had infused the brand with her own personality. Consumers were not simply buying makeup;

they were entering the Charlotte Tilbury universe. That universe promised glamour, transformation, and a touch of theater, but it was always grounded in usability. The balance between aspiration and practicality was her winning formula.

For industry observers, the Selfridges launch also represented a turning point in how luxury beauty brands connected with customers. Charlotte Tilbury Beauty was built at the intersection of artistry, education, and commerce. She understood that modern consumers wanted to be shown how to use products, not just to admire them from afar. The inclusion of tutorial cards, videos, and staff trained to demonstrate looks reinforced that her brand was about guidance as much as it was about glamour.

The immediate press reception reflected the brand's impact. *Vogue*, *The Telegraph*, and other major outlets ran features highlighting both Charlotte's background and the promise of her new venture. Reviews praised the quality of the products, noting that they delivered on performance while also carrying the polish of high-end beauty. Critics emphasized that her credibility as a makeup artist gave the line a level of authenticity often missing from celebrity-led or corporate-launched beauty ranges.

In the weeks following the launch, demand exceeded expectations. Products sold out quickly at Selfridges, and restocks were met with equal enthusiasm. Consumers began sharing their experiences online, particularly praising the clarity of the looks system and the effectiveness of key products like the Filmstar Bronze & Glow palette and the Full Fat Lashes mascara. The online buzz amplified the brand's visibility, reaching audiences beyond London and setting the stage for wider expansion.

For Charlotte herself, the launch was a validation of her vision. She had identified a gap in the luxury beauty market where consumers wanted products that carried both prestige and practicality, and she had filled it. The brand immediately stood apart from its competitors by offering an entire philosophy of beauty rather than just a set of products. This holistic approach turned customers into loyalists, and loyalists into ambassadors who spread the word.

Charlotte Tilbury biography

What is most striking about that moment in 2013 is how carefully Charlotte had timed her entry. The luxury beauty sector was crowded, with heritage brands dominating department store counters, but none had fully embraced the combination of artistry, storytelling, and education in the way she did. By merging her credibility as an artist with the accessibility of curated looks, she positioned her brand as something both new and trustworthy. The industry took notice, and the competition would eventually adapt, but Charlotte Tilbury Beauty had already secured its place as an innovator.

Looking back, the founding of Charlotte Tilbury Beauty in 2013 was more than just the creation of another cosmetics line. It was the moment a makeup artist transformed her craft into a global business blueprint. By launching at Selfridges with a collection designed to empower, guide, and excite consumers, Charlotte captured the imagination of the public and set the tone for what her brand would become in the years that followed. The combination of strong storytelling, product excellence, and customer connection gave her an edge that could not be ignored, and it began in that single launch that brought professional artistry into the hands of everyday consumers.

The impact of that launch reverberated far beyond the counters at Selfridges. It marked the arrival of a new kind of beauty brand, one that was both luxurious and approachable, aspirational yet grounded in artistry. For Charlotte Tilbury, it was the realization of a vision she had been shaping for years, and for the industry, it was the beginning of a new era in how beauty was imagined, sold, and experienced.

Chapter 10: Product Icons and Bestsellers

From the moment Charlotte Tilbury launched her namesake brand in 2013, she made it clear that her vision for beauty would not be confined to fleeting trends or seasonal experiments. Her approach to product creation was personal, rooted in the practical demands of her years as a professional makeup artist and elevated by her unrelenting pursuit of perfection. The result was a line of cosmetics and skincare that combined artistry with accessibility, performance with glamour. Over time, a few creations would transcend the brand's growing catalogue to become cultural touchstones—products that carried their own mythology, defined makeup looks across continents, and solidified Charlotte Tilbury Beauty as one of the most influential names in modern luxury cosmetics.

Among these, none have left a mark quite like the Pillow Talk collection, a phenomenon that turned a single lipstick shade into an entire world of beauty storytelling. Alongside it, the Magic Cream stood as a backstage secret that evolved into a skincare legend, while the company's carefully curated lipsticks, eyeshadow palettes, and complexion products formed the foundation of an empire that continues to expand in 2025. Together, these icons did more than sell millions of units; they reshaped how beauty is marketed, experienced, and remembered.

When Pillow Talk first appeared in 2013, it was conceived as a universal nude-pink lipstick—something that could enhance the natural lip color of almost anyone who wore it. Tilbury drew on her years of experience working with models, celebrities, and everyday women to create a tone that balanced warmth and neutrality in perfect proportion. The shade was originally introduced as part of her Matte Revolution Lipstick line, a formula she had spent considerable time refining for both texture and wearability. Its matte finish, unlike the flat dryness typical of other products in the category, delivered a velvety softness that felt as luxurious as it looked.

The name Pillow Talk captured something deeper than a color; it suggested intimacy, confidence, and allure. It was marketing and emotion perfectly intertwined. When the lipstick launched at Selfridges in London, it sold out within days. Customers who tried it often spoke about its adaptability—how it seemed to adjust subtly to different skin tones and lighting, appearing pinker on some and more neutral on others. That flexibility turned it into a universal favorite, something rare in an industry where shades are often constrained by complexion categories.

As social media gained momentum, Pillow Talk found its second wave of fame. Makeup artists, influencers, and celebrities began to share tutorials and selfies featuring the lipstick, pushing it from cult favorite to mainstream icon. What made the phenomenon even more remarkable was its longevity. Most products experience short-lived success, yet Pillow Talk continued to dominate bestseller lists year after year. By 2017, it had become the cornerstone of a full collection, with Tilbury expanding the line to include lip liners, blushes, and eyeshadow palettes under the same name.

The expansion worked because Pillow Talk had become more than a shade; it had become an aesthetic—a language of soft, romantic glamour that consumers could adapt to their personal style. In 2020,

Charlotte Tilbury biography

Tilbury introduced Pillow Talk Medium and Pillow Talk Intense, acknowledging the need for inclusivity and broader skin tone representation. These additions allowed more customers to find their perfect version of the original hue, reinforcing the brand's commitment to universality while keeping the core emotion intact. By 2025, Pillow Talk had evolved into a multi-category franchise covering lips, eyes, cheeks, and complexion, each launch generating anticipation across beauty publications and digital communities.

Its impact on the business was transformative. Pillow Talk was not just a bestseller; it was a blueprint for how modern beauty could merge product innovation with storytelling. Every launch carried Tilbury's voice, her descriptions rich with theatrical flair—phrases like "the secret to the perfect pout" or "dreamy pink perfection" turned product pages into stage scripts. Her marketing balanced accessibility with aspiration, allowing customers to feel they were part of something luxurious yet attainable. The consistency of messaging, combined with genuine product performance, created a cycle of trust rarely seen in contemporary beauty retail.

Charlotte Tilbury biography

If Pillow Talk represented the glamour of lips, the Magic Cream embodied the science of skin. Its story began long before the brand existed, in the backstage chaos of fashion shows and editorial shoots. Tilbury often found herself needing to revive tired, dehydrated skin on models who had endured long flights or hours of makeup applications. Around the year 2000, she began experimenting with her own blend of moisturizers, mixing active ingredients like hyaluronic acid, rosehip oil, and peptides to create what she called her "magic" formula.

The cream became legendary among those who worked with her. Models would request it by name before major shows, calling it "Charlotte's Magic Cream." For years, it was an insider's secret, a backstage staple without a label. When Tilbury prepared to launch her brand, it was inevitable that this product would become one of its pillars. The Magic Cream officially debuted in 2013 as part of the initial product lineup, and much like Pillow Talk, it immediately developed a devoted following.

Charlotte Tilbury biography

What set it apart from other moisturizers was both its texture and its philosophy. Tilbury often emphasized that skincare was the foundation of any great makeup look. She saw Magic Cream as the first step in transforming skin before any brush or foundation came near it. Its formula was rich yet quick-absorbing, designed to plump and smooth the skin while imparting a natural luminosity. The scent—a blend of floral and slightly powdery notes—added an element of ritual to its use.

The product's appeal was also tied to its authenticity. It wasn't created in a laboratory to fit a market gap; it was born from years of real-world experience. Tilbury frequently demonstrated its use in tutorials, massaging it into the skin with her "Tilbury Tap" technique, a rhythmic motion meant to stimulate circulation and enhance radiance. These small, personal details gave the Magic Cream an aura of intimacy, bridging professional expertise and consumer experience.

Over time, the line expanded to include variations such as Magic Eye Rescue and Magic Night Cream, each designed to complement the original. In 2022, Charlotte Tilbury Beauty introduced Magic Water Cream, a lightweight version aimed at customers seeking hydration without heaviness. The innovation demonstrated how the brand continuously refined its core offerings while responding to consumer needs. Magic Cream remains one of the most awarded moisturizers in the beauty industry, with consistent recognition for its efficacy and luxurious feel.

If Pillow Talk and Magic Cream defined the brand's soul, the broader collection of lipsticks, palettes, and skincare innovations gave it enduring structure. Tilbury's approach to product development combined the discipline of a makeup artist with the intuition of a storyteller. Each item was conceived not in isolation but as part of an interconnected system—a "wardrobe of beauty," as she often described it. Customers could mix and match products to create complete looks, much like assembling an outfit.

Her lipstick ranges, in particular, reflected this philosophy. Beyond Pillow Talk, the Matte Revolution and K.I.S.S.I.N.G lines offered a spectrum of shades inspired by icons, moods, and timeless glamour. The formulations prioritized comfort without sacrificing payoff, a balance that appealed to professionals and everyday users alike. The shade Walk of No Shame, originally launched as Walk of Shame in 2014, became another enduring favorite, celebrated for its flattering berry-rose tone and empowering message.

Eyeshadows formed another pillar of her artistry. Tilbury understood that eyes are the emotional center of the face, and her palettes were designed to simplify professional techniques for the consumer. The Luxury Palette series introduced quads organized by theme—each compact containing four coordinated shades labeled Prime, Enhance, Smoke, and Pop. This structure guided users through the process of building dimension with ease, demystifying the artistry behind editorial looks. Standout releases like the Dolce Vita Palette, later renamed Bella Sofia, and the Golden Goddess Palette became staples in beauty collections worldwide.

In 2019, Tilbury released the Pillow Talk Instant Eye Palette, a 12-shade expansion that extended the original lip color's universe into the eyes. It sold out almost instantly upon release, underscoring how deeply the

Charlotte Tilbury biography

Pillow Talk aesthetic had embedded itself in popular culture. By consistently linking new products to recognizable narratives, Tilbury ensured that each launch built on the success of the last.

Her innovations extended into complexion and skincare, bridging the gap between makeup and treatment. Products like the Hollywood Flawless Filter, introduced in 2018, blurred the boundaries between highlighter, primer, and foundation enhancer. Inspired by the glowing skin of actresses under soft-focus lighting, it became one of the brand's most talked-about launches. By 2024, it had inspired numerous imitations across the industry, but Tilbury's version remained unmatched in texture and finish.

The Charlotte's Beautiful Skin Foundation, released in 2022, marked another turning point. It reflected her understanding that modern consumers valued both coverage and care. The foundation was infused with hyaluronic acid and rose complex, promising hydration alongside a natural finish. Reviews consistently highlighted its versatility across skin types and its ability to maintain luminosity throughout the day. Paired with the Beautiful Skin Sun-Kissed Glow Bronzer and the Airbrush Flawless Finish powder, Tilbury's complexion range achieved cult status, balancing performance with a luxury experience.

Innovation at Charlotte Tilbury Beauty was never limited to formulas; it extended to packaging and presentation. The brand's design language—deep rose-gold hues, star motifs, and art deco influences—created instant visual identity. The tactile quality of the compacts and tubes reinforced the sense of indulgence. Customers often described using the products as a form of self-care, not merely application. This emotional connection transformed beauty routines into daily rituals.

Skincare innovations continued to strengthen the brand's foundation. The Magic Serum Crystal Elixir, launched in 2020, introduced active ingredients like vitamin C, niacinamide, and polyglutamic acid to support brightness and texture. Its release reflected Tilbury's increasing investment in the science of skincare, aligning her brand with clinical credibility while maintaining its signature glamour. In 2023, the

Glow Toner further expanded the skincare line, offering exfoliation and radiance enhancement through a gentle acid blend.

Behind each of these launches lay a meticulous process. Tilbury's product development was collaborative but tightly controlled. She remained involved in testing and refining textures, shades, and performance metrics, often referencing the demands she had encountered during her years as a makeup artist. Every new addition had to meet both artistic and commercial standards. The brand's R&D team worked closely with chemists to translate Tilbury's creative direction into tangible results, ensuring consistency and innovation coexisted.

By 2025, Charlotte Tilbury Beauty's catalogue represented a balance of continuity and evolution. While Pillow Talk and Magic Cream continued to anchor the lineup, newer innovations reflected the brand's adaptability in an increasingly competitive market. Seasonal releases maintained excitement, but the enduring appeal of the core products demonstrated something rarer: genuine loyalty. Customers did not

Charlotte Tilbury biography

move on from Tilbury's icons; they built collections around them.

The business impact of these products was immense. Industry analysts credited Pillow Talk alone with driving significant annual revenue growth and sustaining global recognition. Magic Cream remained one of the top-selling moisturizers in luxury retail, while her complexion products consistently topped charts in multiple regions. But beyond numbers, the influence of these creations lay in how they redefined consumer expectations.

Tilbury had proven that luxury could be both aspirational and approachable, that a brand rooted in artistry could speak directly to individuals. Each product told a story—a promise of transformation supported by visible results. In doing so, she bridged the emotional and practical dimensions of beauty, creating a model that many others have since tried to emulate.

As 2025 continues, the icons of Charlotte Tilbury Beauty remain as relevant as the day they were introduced. The Pillow Talk line continues to expand, with new limited editions and seasonal interpretations

Charlotte Tilbury biography

capturing consumer imagination. Magic Cream stands unchanged in its essential form, a reminder that true innovation endures. The lipsticks, palettes, and skincare innovations that followed have become not just products but symbols of an era in beauty defined by creativity, inclusivity, and the power of vision.

Through them, Charlotte Tilbury achieved what few in her field have managed: the creation of timeless beauty artifacts that speak as powerfully to professional artists as to those discovering makeup for the first time. Each item is a chapter in a continuing narrative—a story of transformation told through color, texture, and the confidence they inspire. In the world she built, beauty is not a mask but a medium, and the icons she created remain its most eloquent expression.

Chapter 11: Global Expansion and Flagship Stores

When Charlotte Tilbury launched her beauty brand in 2013, the makeup industry was already crowded with legacy names and luxury labels that had dominated for decades. Yet from the beginning, she believed that her company could carve out something distinct—a brand that merged artistry and accessibility, glamour and education, and product and personality. That conviction soon became the foundation for one of the most significant expansion stories in modern beauty. Within just a few years, Charlotte Tilbury Beauty evolved from a single launch counter in London's Selfridges to a global presence spanning Europe, the United States, the Middle East, and Asia. The pace and precision of this growth were not accidental; they were the result of clear creative vision paired with a keen understanding of retail strategy in a rapidly digitizing world.

The initial phase of expansion began close to home. After the success of her 2013 Selfridges debut, Tilbury quickly moved to solidify her footprint across the United

Charlotte Tilbury biography

Kingdom. Her products were introduced in major British department stores, including Harrods, Harvey Nichols, and Fenwick. Each counter mirrored the brand's signature aesthetic—rich rose-gold tones, art-deco inspired mirrors, and lighting designed to make every customer feel like they were stepping into a professional dressing room. The consistent visual identity helped reinforce brand recall, something Tilbury understood deeply from her years in fashion and editorial work. By 2015, the brand's British retail presence was robust enough to support international expansion, and plans for global rollout were already in motion.

Europe provided a natural starting point. The brand's ethos of glamour and empowerment resonated with European consumers who valued artistry and narrative as much as product quality. In 2015, Charlotte Tilbury Beauty expanded into key European markets, opening dedicated spaces in cities such as Paris, Amsterdam, and Milan. These locations were chosen carefully—not just for sales potential but for their influence within fashion and beauty culture. The Paris expansion, in particular, was seen as both symbolic and strategic: it marked the brand's entry into the birthplace of haute couture and luxury cosmetics. Tilbury's personal credibility as an internationally recognized makeup artist allowed her to introduce her line not as an outsider, but as an insider offering her expertise in product form.

The United States represented a different kind of challenge and opportunity. American consumers were driven by trends and social media influence, and Tilbury recognized that a digital-first approach would be key to success there. In 2016, the brand made its U.S. debut through partnerships with high-end retailers, first with Nordstrom and later with Bloomingdale's and Bergdorf Goodman. That same year, Charlotte Tilbury opened her first standalone U.S. store in Los Angeles at The Grove. The location choice reflected both Hollywood's deep connection to beauty culture and the city's global reputation for trendsetting. The store embodied the full Charlotte Tilbury experience: makeup stations for on-the-spot transformations, custom lighting to replicate different environments, and staff trained to deliver the same energy Tilbury brought to her backstage makeup chairs.

Charlotte Tilbury biography

From there, the brand's American expansion accelerated. In 2017, Charlotte Tilbury counters appeared in Sephora locations across the country, dramatically increasing visibility. Her products' blend of luxury presentation and easy-to-use formulations resonated strongly with U.S. shoppers who wanted high performance without intimidation. The brand's storytelling—built around looks such as "The Golden Goddess" and "The Rock Chick"—translated seamlessly into the American market. The clarity of these personas made it simple for consumers to identify with the brand's message of confidence through makeup.

The Middle East soon followed as a natural extension of Tilbury's expansion strategy. By 2018, her brand had entered Dubai and other major cities across the region. The Middle Eastern market was known for its love of luxury and glamour, two qualities central to the Charlotte Tilbury aesthetic. The brand partnered with retail groups familiar with regional tastes, ensuring cultural alignment and premium positioning. Store designs were adapted to reflect the opulence expected in Middle Eastern shopping destinations while maintaining the core visual

Charlotte Tilbury biography

DNA recognizable to customers worldwide. The response was immediate. Customers connected not only with the quality of the products but with Tilbury's overarching message: that makeup could be empowering, transformative, and universally appealing.

Asia represented a more complex but equally crucial chapter in the brand's international story. The rise of beauty consumerism in China, South Korea, and Japan during the late 2010s offered enormous potential. In 2019, Charlotte Tilbury Beauty launched on Tmall Global, Alibaba's international e-commerce platform, marking the brand's formal entry into the Chinese market. The digital-first launch reflected a deep understanding of local consumer behavior, where online discovery and influencer-driven marketing were far more influential than traditional retail. Social platforms like Weibo and Xiaohongshu became essential channels for building brand awareness. Tilbury's emphasis on skin-perfecting products, such as the Hollywood Flawless Filter and Airbrush Flawless Foundation, resonated with Asian beauty consumers who valued luminous, camera-ready finishes.

Charlotte Tilbury biography

Following the success of the online rollout, physical retail locations across Asia soon followed. Flagship stores were established in Hong Kong, Seoul, and Singapore. These stores were more than sales points; they were designed as immersive environments that communicated Tilbury's creative world. Mirrors framed in soft rose gold, velvet seating, and "Tilbury Transformations" stations created a sense of theater. Each store was staffed with makeup artists trained to replicate the brand's approach to beauty consultation—personalized, aspirational, and celebratory.

While the physical retail expansion was impressive, the brand's digital strategy proved equally important in maintaining growth momentum. From its inception, Charlotte Tilbury Beauty was built with a strong online presence. Tilbury had recognized early that digital storytelling would be vital to building a global community. Her official website became both a retail hub and an educational platform. Detailed tutorials, virtual try-on tools, and look-based shopping experiences allowed users to engage with products as if guided by Tilbury herself.

This digital-first mindset distinguished her brand from many traditional luxury houses that were slower to adapt. By 2020, the company had fully integrated augmented reality tools and personalized recommendations, enhancing customer engagement at a time when the COVID-19 pandemic disrupted in-person shopping. Virtual consultations with trained makeup artists became a cornerstone of the brand's customer service strategy. The transition felt seamless because the groundwork had been laid years earlier. These innovations not only sustained the brand through global uncertainty but expanded its audience.

As online retail grew, the physical flagship stores evolved to serve a different role. They became experience centers—destinations rather than simple shops. The London flagship on Covent Garden, which opened in 2015, remained the model of how Charlotte Tilbury envisioned her brand in a physical space. The boutique was designed as a beauty theater, complete with an "Instant Magic Facial" room and dedicated zones for signature looks. Every element—from lighting temperature to scent—was calibrated to create emotional engagement. The store became a regular feature in London's luxury retail landscape, drawing both tourists and locals.

New flagships opened in the years that followed, each tailored to its city while maintaining brand consistency. The Dubai Mall boutique embodied regional luxury with marble details and private consultation suites. The Hong Kong flagship emphasized innovation, featuring digital mirrors that allowed customers to preview makeup looks. The Los Angeles location leaned into Hollywood glamour, hosting events with celebrities and influencers. These spaces reinforced the brand's narrative of beauty as experience, not just transaction.

Expansion across continents demanded logistical sophistication and consistent quality control. Charlotte Tilbury Beauty developed centralized product distribution and localized marketing teams to ensure alignment across markets. The company's partnership with Puig in 2020 accelerated this structure, providing greater operational reach while preserving Tilbury's creative authority. It also opened access to Puig's global supply chain, enabling faster rollout of products and campaigns across multiple territories.

By 2021, the brand's online and offline networks were fully integrated. Campaigns launched simultaneously across markets, supported by consistent visuals and storytelling. One notable example was the global campaign for the Airbrush Flawless Foundation, which featured models of diverse backgrounds and was adapted into multiple languages. The uniform presentation strengthened brand identity while allowing for cultural flexibility.

Charlotte Tilbury's retail expansion coincided with a growing movement in beauty retail towards inclusivity and personalization. She positioned her brand as one that could serve all ages and skin tones without diluting its luxury positioning. Her counters and boutiques were designed to feel welcoming rather than intimidating, an approach that resonated strongly in emerging markets. By 2022, the brand's retail footprint spanned more than 50 countries, and its products were available online in over 120.

Charlotte Tilbury biography

The year 2023 brought further developments as Charlotte Tilbury Beauty deepened its presence in Asia. The brand launched localized e-commerce platforms in Japan and South Korea, offering region-specific shipping and customer service. These moves reflected a deliberate effort to blend global consistency with local relevance. In addition, the company invested heavily in live-streaming commerce, a dominant trend in Asian markets. Charlotte Tilbury herself appeared in several broadcasts, maintaining the personal connection that remained central to her brand's appeal.

As part of its continued expansion strategy, the company focused on sustainability within its retail and packaging design. By 2024, many of the flagship stores incorporated eco-conscious materials, and the brand introduced refillable packaging for several bestsellers. These initiatives reflected growing consumer awareness around environmental responsibility and demonstrated Tilbury's commitment to evolving with her audience.

The success of this global network rested on maintaining authenticity. Each boutique, whether in London, Dubai, New York, or Hong Kong, offered a consistent sense of theater, intimacy, and luxury. Yet the true unifying factor across regions remained Tilbury's personality—her unmistakable enthusiasm for transformation and self-belief. Customers worldwide recognized the same spirit that had made her famous as a makeup artist: the conviction that beauty was about empowerment.

By 2025, Charlotte Tilbury Beauty had established itself as one of the leading global luxury beauty brands. Its combination of immersive flagship experiences and sophisticated digital ecosystems allowed it to compete with the largest and oldest players in the industry. The company's flagship stores had become landmarks in their own right, attracting visitors as much for inspiration as for shopping. The Covent Garden store in London continued to be a symbol of the brand's origins, while new boutiques across Asia and the United States embodied its future.

Through these expansions, Tilbury achieved something rare in modern beauty: a brand that felt both personal and global. The same vision that guided her from makeup chair to retail counter now shaped her empire's worldwide presence. Every store opening, every online campaign, and every market entry carried the same message she had championed since the beginning—that makeup is not just about appearance but about confidence, joy, and transformation.

Charlotte Tilbury's global expansion was more than a business strategy; it was the extension of her creative philosophy onto a world stage. From Europe to the Americas, from the Middle East to Asia, each step reinforced her belief that glamour could be universal. Her brand's journey across borders stood as proof that beauty, when built on authenticity and imagination, knows no boundaries.

Chapter 12: Accolades and Industry Partnerships

When Charlotte Tilbury launched her beauty brand in 2013, she did not simply introduce a new line of cosmetics; she unveiled a complete philosophy of glamour that redefined how luxury beauty could be marketed, packaged, and experienced. As the brand gained momentum, its trajectory was propelled by strategic partnerships with major retailers, an impressive array of international awards, and the establishment of a marketing identity that became inseparable from Tilbury herself. These achievements, though diverse in form, shared one foundation: a clear, consistent vision of what modern luxury should feel like.

By 2014, the success of her Selfridges debut had created unprecedented demand beyond the United Kingdom. Beauty consumers across Europe and the United States were increasingly drawn to the brand's storytelling approach—products that promised not just enhancement, but transformation. Recognizing this momentum, Tilbury pursued alliances with global retail partners whose reach and reputation could match her ambitions. One of the earliest and most defining of these was her collaboration with *Net-a-Porter*, the luxury online retailer known for curating high-end fashion and beauty brands.

The partnership with Net-a-Porter began in 2015 and symbolized a crucial evolution in how luxury cosmetics were sold online. While many beauty houses hesitated to fully embrace digital retail, Tilbury saw it as a natural extension of her brand's mission to empower and educate through accessibility. Net-a-Porter, already trusted by an affluent global customer base, provided the perfect digital showcase. The collaboration allowed her to blend prestige with convenience, reaching consumers who valued immediacy but expected sophistication. The curated product presentations on the platform, featuring her bestsellers like Magic Cream, Filmstar Bronze & Glow, and the Pillow Talk lipstick, mirrored the editorial elegance that had defined Tilbury's career in fashion.

The partnership was not just about distribution; it was a statement of positioning. Tilbury's products sat alongside brands such as Tom Ford Beauty and La Mer, reinforcing her arrival in the highest echelons of the luxury beauty world. The relationship also emphasized her understanding of the digital landscape, a skill that would continue to distinguish her brand in an industry where traditional prestige houses were still learning to adapt. Net-a-Porter benefited equally, as Tilbury's ability to create excitement around new launches and limited editions drove engagement and traffic.

Following the success of her collaboration with Net-a-Porter, Tilbury set her sights on broadening her physical presence. The global cosmetics market was evolving rapidly, with consumer habits shifting toward seamless omnichannel experiences that combined online shopping with in-store discovery. In 2016, Charlotte Tilbury Beauty entered *Sephora*, a milestone that placed the brand at the center of the world's most influential beauty retail network.

Sephora's reputation for blending mass appeal with luxury credibility made it an ideal partner. For Tilbury, whose brand message championed both artistry and accessibility, this collaboration opened new opportunities to connect with beauty enthusiasts in North America,

Charlotte Tilbury biography

Europe, and later in Asia. The rollout was meticulously planned, beginning with select flagship stores before expanding across multiple markets. Sephora's immersive retail model—offering personalized consultations, tutorials, and product sampling—aligned perfectly with Tilbury's philosophy of hands-on glamour.

What set these partnerships apart was not merely their commercial success but the deliberate care with which Tilbury integrated her brand identity into each new environment. Whether online or in a physical boutique, the signature rose-gold packaging, Hollywood-inspired product names, and empowering marketing language remained consistent. This uniformity created a sense of reliability and aspiration, transforming every retail touchpoint into an extension of her world. By maintaining aesthetic control while scaling distribution, Tilbury managed to achieve what many luxury founders struggle to sustain: growth without dilution.

As the brand expanded, accolades from the beauty and design industries began to accumulate, affirming both the creative and technical excellence behind its products. In 2015, *Charlotte Tilbury Beauty* received the *CEW*

Charlotte Tilbury biography

(Cosmetic Executive Women) Award for Best New Brand, an honor that recognized not only product innovation but also the brand's cultural impact within its first two years of existence. The CEW recognition held particular weight in the British beauty sector, as it represented peer acknowledgment from professionals across marketing, retail, and artistry.

In subsequent years, specific products earned repeated praise. The *Magic Cream*, which had started as Tilbury's personal backstage secret, won multiple awards for skincare innovation, including *Tatler's Beauty Award* and *Harper's Bazaar's Anti-Aging Award*. The *Pillow Talk Lipstick*, launched in 2017, achieved cult status and was honored by publications such as *Elle* and *Glamour* for its universal tone and long-lasting appeal. What these awards signified went beyond sales figures—they marked the transition of her products into cultural staples. Each recognition reinforced the perception of Tilbury as a tastemaker capable of blending artistry with commercial intuition.

Her approach to packaging design became another pillar of acclaim. The distinctive rose-gold aesthetic, paired with geometric lines inspired by the glamour of 1920s cinema, quickly became one of the most recognizable brand identities in modern beauty. The attention to tactile detail—the satisfying magnetic click of a lipstick tube, the artful symmetry of her compact mirrors—transformed everyday objects into keepsakes. This design philosophy did not go unnoticed. Industry organizations and design juries highlighted her packaging for its combination of functionality and visual storytelling. The *Pentawards*, one of the world's leading design competitions, acknowledged her brand's exceptional presentation, citing how it evoked timeless luxury while maintaining a sense of modernity.

Tilbury's accolades also extended to her leadership. In 2016, she received the *Fashion Retail Academy's Outstanding Achievement Award*, celebrating her influence as both a creative force and a business innovator. In 2018, when she was named a Member of the Order of the British Empire (MBE) by Queen Elizabeth II, the honor marked an important moment of national recognition. The distinction reflected her dual role as an artist and entrepreneur who had contributed significantly to Britain's global reputation for excellence in fashion and beauty.

Despite the growing list of honors, Tilbury never treated awards as mere symbols of prestige. They functioned as markers of credibility, strengthening her relationships with retailers, media partners, and collaborators. The recognition reinforced consumer trust and demonstrated that behind the glamour lay rigorous standards of quality and innovation.

As her reputation soared, Tilbury became increasingly adept at forming partnerships that transcended traditional beauty boundaries. Her collaborations with major retailers were strategic not only in reach but also in alignment with her long-term vision. Beyond Net-a-Porter and Sephora, the brand established successful relationships with *Harrods*, *Selfridges*, *Nordstrom*, and *Bloomingdale's*, creating a network of distribution that balanced exclusivity with accessibility. Each retailer served a distinct purpose. Harrods, for instance, embodied British prestige; Sephora provided global exposure; and Net-a-Porter bridged digital luxury with editorial sophistication. Together, they constructed a retail architecture that reflected Tilbury's multifaceted approach to brand-building.

Between 2017 and 2020, *Charlotte Tilbury Beauty* continued to receive honors that emphasized its strength as a modern luxury powerhouse. The *Sunday Times Virgin Fast Track 100* listed the company among Britain's fastest-growing private firms, underscoring its commercial vitality. Business publications began profiling Tilbury not only as a creative visionary but also as a CEO whose leadership fused intuition with strategic precision. Her ability to identify cultural trends and translate them into tangible business outcomes distinguished her from many peers in the crowded beauty sector.

As the company matured, its marketing strategy evolved into a masterclass in luxury storytelling. Tilbury's campaigns consistently blurred the line between artistry and aspiration. Each product launch was treated as an event, often accompanied by cinematic videos, glamorous global premieres, and appearances by celebrity muses such as Kate Moss, Amal Clooney, and Phoebe Dynevor. Rather than relying on abstract imagery, the brand's communication emphasized empowerment—inviting women to feel confident, radiant, and unstoppable.

By 2019, *Charlotte Tilbury Beauty* had become synonymous with modern luxury marketing. This was not achieved through the detached minimalism that defined other high-end beauty houses, but through warmth and personality. The language was direct yet uplifting, combining expert authority with friendliness. Campaigns used phrases like "Give yourself the Tilbury glow" and "Darlings, it's all about confidence," which became instantly recognizable. This tone mirrored Charlotte's own presence in public appearances and digital content, where she often addressed customers directly with genuine enthusiasm.

The brand's integration of storytelling, aesthetics, and community engagement soon made it a case study for how personality-driven marketing could thrive in a digital economy. The *British Fashion Council* and marketing analysts highlighted her success in connecting emotional resonance with commercial performance. Unlike traditional luxury advertising that emphasized

Charlotte Tilbury biography

distance, Tilbury's approach centered on inclusion—she made luxury feel attainable without stripping it of its allure.

Awards for innovation continued to follow this marketing success. In 2021, her company was recognized at the *CEW Beauty Awards* for *Best Social Media Campaign*, celebrating its ability to merge creative storytelling with measurable business impact. The same year, *Charlotte's Magic Serum Crystal Elixir* received praise for its scientific formulation, bridging skincare technology with luxury branding. Industry reports cited how Tilbury's marketing combined data-driven precision with the emotional clarity of a personal conversation, setting a standard that many competitors would later emulate.

The brand's retail partnerships grew stronger in this period, particularly through exclusive collaborations that elevated both Tilbury and her partners. With *Sephora*, she introduced global limited-edition kits designed to celebrate milestones and holidays, turning product launches into cultural events. With *Net-a-Porter*, she pioneered curated digital experiences that blended editorial storytelling with purchase opportunities. Each collaboration was designed not only to boost sales but to enhance customer engagement through immersive experiences.

In 2022, as the brand entered its tenth year, Charlotte Tilbury Beauty was recognized by *WWD Beauty Inc.* with the *Brand of the Year* award, acknowledging its sustained influence on the global market. The citation praised its consistency in innovation, cohesive identity, and leadership in modern beauty retail. It marked a decade of transformation that had begun with a single counter in London and grown into a global network spanning dozens of countries.

Tilbury's approach to partnerships remained grounded in selectivity. She collaborated only with entities that aligned with her values of excellence, artistry, and inclusivity. When the Spanish luxury group Puig acquired a majority stake in her company in 2020, she ensured the partnership maintained creative independence. This balance of artistic control with corporate scale allowed the brand to preserve authenticity while expanding reach. Her insistence on maintaining her team's creative freedom was widely respected within the industry, reinforcing her image as both visionary and protector of her brand's integrity.

By 2023, Charlotte Tilbury's influence in beauty marketing had transcended her own brand. She became a sought-after speaker and panelist at international conferences, discussing the future of luxury branding, digital retail, and women's leadership. Business schools and marketing analysts cited her strategies as examples of how storytelling, inclusivity, and brand consistency could drive success in a saturated market. Awards from *Forbes* and *Marie Claire* recognized her as one of the most powerful women in beauty, cementing her position not just as an entrepreneur but as a thought leader shaping the global conversation around beauty and identity.

Through it all, the foundation of her achievements remained rooted in the same principles that had guided her from the start: craftsmanship, charisma, and connection. Her collaborations with Net-a-Porter, Sephora, and leading retailers were not mere commercial arrangements but relationships built on shared vision.

Charlotte Tilbury biography

Her awards in innovation and design were not decorative trophies but evidence of a brand culture committed to excellence. And her mastery of luxury marketing did not rely on opulence alone, but on authenticity—the rare ability to make glamour feel both aspirational and human.

By 2025, more than a decade after its founding, *Charlotte Tilbury Beauty* stands as one of the most decorated and admired names in modern cosmetics. The walls of the brand's London headquarters are lined with awards recognizing everything from formulation to packaging, from digital storytelling to entrepreneurship. Yet the truest measure of Tilbury's success lies in how she changed perceptions of what a beauty brand could represent. Her collaborations and accolades tell a story not only of growth but of evolution—a vision of luxury that celebrates artistry, inclusivity, and the enduring power of confidence.

In the constellation of global beauty, Charlotte Tilbury has achieved a balance few manage to sustain: the creative soul of an artist, the discipline of an executive, and the charisma of a modern icon. Through strategic alliances, celebrated designs, and a marketing voice that feels unmistakably her own, she has not merely participated in the evolution of luxury beauty—she has defined it.

PART V: LEADERSHIP, AMBASSADORSHIP, AND INFLUENCE

In an industry defined by trends, Charlotte Tilbury became the trendsetter. Her influence extended far beyond her products, shaping how beauty was communicated, marketed, and experienced across continents. As she transitioned from makeup artist to business leader, she built a brand culture anchored in empowerment and creativity — not just glamour. This part captures how her leadership style, partnerships, and ambassadorial roles elevated both her name and the beauty landscape itself, reflecting a legacy built on innovation, mentorship, and an instinctive understanding of what makes people feel confident.

Chapter 13: Beauty Advocate and Industry Ambassador

When Charlotte Tilbury walked into Buckingham Palace on February 20, 2019, to officially receive her appointment as a Member of the Order of the British Empire (MBE) for services to the beauty and cosmetics industry, the honor was more than ceremonial recognition. It was a public acknowledgment that her influence extended well beyond brushes, pigments, and the polished image of a luxury brand. By the time Queen Elizabeth II conferred the award, Tilbury had already transformed herself into a cultural figurehead, one whose work bridged entrepreneurship, creative expression, and international advocacy. The recognition reflected both her personal achievements and her ability to champion beauty as a serious industry within the global economy.

The path to that day had been carefully built over years of consistent contributions, not only through her artistry but also through her dedication to promoting creativity and female entrepreneurship. Receiving an MBE was a deeply symbolic moment. For a profession often seen as secondary or superficial in comparison with fashion or fine art, the honor validated beauty as a legitimate sector of cultural and economic power. Tilbury became part of a select group of creative professionals whose work was seen as vital to Britain's international image.

The MBE also positioned her publicly as more than a founder of a successful brand. It identified her as a voice and advocate for an industry that had traditionally been dismissed or underestimated. For Tilbury, this acknowledgment underscored her mission to elevate beauty into broader conversations about business, innovation, and culture. Her acceptance speech reflected gratitude not only for her team but also for the global community of women who supported her brand and embraced the ethos of confidence she consistently promoted. It was a recognition that beauty, in her philosophy, was not a trivial accessory but a tool for empowerment and self-expression.

From that moment, her role as a formal ambassador for the beauty industry began to take shape in a way that was both official and deeply personal. In interviews following the investiture, Tilbury emphasized her desire to inspire women to pursue entrepreneurship without fear, drawing from her own journey as a businesswoman who built a company from the ground up. Her message resonated with aspiring entrepreneurs who saw in her success a model of how creativity could be transformed into a thriving enterprise.

Tilbury's advocacy for female entrepreneurship has been a consistent theme of her public life. She has often spoken about the barriers women face in business, whether through limited access to funding, societal expectations, or a lack of mentorship opportunities. Her company became not just a vehicle for selling products but a platform for championing the potential of women to lead and innovate. In panel discussions, keynote speeches, and brand initiatives, she framed beauty as a professional path worthy of recognition, encouraging young women to consider it a space where they could excel both artistically and commercially.

In 2019, the year she received her MBE, Tilbury amplified her advocacy through appearances at major business and creative forums. She participated in conferences where she discussed the intersection of

Charlotte Tilbury biography

entrepreneurship and creativity, offering her own brand as a case study of how a personal passion could evolve into a global powerhouse. She repeatedly pointed out that the beauty industry contributed significantly to the British economy and deserved recognition equal to other creative industries such as fashion, film, and design. This insistence placed her at the forefront of conversations about how governments and institutions could better support beauty professionals.

Her leadership extended beyond the stage. Within her company, she created structures designed to empower women in leadership positions. The majority of her brand's workforce has consistently been female, with a significant number of women holding executive and managerial roles. This internal culture reflected her external advocacy, reinforcing her message that the path to empowerment was not just theoretical but actively practiced within her own organization.

Tilbury's role as an ambassador also developed in the international arena. Her appointment as MBE gave her added credibility when speaking about British creativity on the global stage. She became a representative of the

Charlotte Tilbury biography

United Kingdom's creative industries in markets where beauty was growing rapidly, including Asia and the Middle East. During brand launches and international tours, she frequently spoke of the importance of British innovation, positioning her own company as part of a larger national story of creativity and excellence.

This global advocacy was particularly visible during trade missions and cultural events supported by the UK government. Tilbury was often cited as a figure who exemplified the potential of British entrepreneurship, especially in industries dominated by heritage houses from France and the United States. Her success story offered an alternative narrative: that a British-born brand could stand at the center of global beauty culture and compete with legacy giants. In doing so, she provided inspiration not only for fellow entrepreneurs but also for the broader perception of Britain's role in the luxury sector.

Her ambassadorship was not limited to commerce and creativity alone. Tilbury consistently emphasized the emotional and social impact of beauty. She argued that makeup and skincare could play a significant role in self-confidence, with implications for mental health and personal empowerment. By framing beauty as both an economic and human force, she widened the scope of her advocacy, making her message resonate beyond the confines of industry insiders.

This message was particularly powerful during events such as International Women's Day, where she frequently highlighted stories of women who used beauty as a stepping stone toward empowerment in their personal and professional lives. Whether speaking to aspiring makeup artists or to established executives, her central message remained consistent: beauty was not frivolous but transformative.

By 2020, when the Spanish fashion and fragrance company Puig acquired a majority stake in Charlotte Tilbury Beauty, her role as an advocate and ambassador became even more pronounced. With the backing of a global luxury group, she had greater reach to amplify her message across continents. Yet she maintained a focus on female empowerment, using her growing platform to spotlight women's achievements and encourage inclusive practices in business.

Charlotte Tilbury biography

The years following her MBE appointment saw her expand this advocacy through structured initiatives. In 2021, she participated in discussions about how digital platforms could democratize entrepreneurship, pointing out how social media allowed women from diverse backgrounds to build brands and reach audiences without the traditional barriers of retail access. Her perspective was informed by her own early embrace of digital platforms, but it also reflected her commitment to championing tools that could empower others.

Her ambassadorship was reinforced in 2022 when she engaged with programs designed to mentor emerging talent in the beauty sector. While many luxury founders maintained distance from grassroots initiatives, Tilbury actively positioned herself as someone invested in the next generation of creatives. This hands-on involvement distinguished her role, showing that her advocacy was not confined to high-level speeches but extended to direct mentorship and support.

In 2023, her international role was once again highlighted when she represented British beauty during campaigns in the United States and Asia. These appearances combined commercial objectives with cultural advocacy, reinforcing the idea that beauty was part of Britain's export identity. Tilbury's presence in these markets was accompanied by consistent messaging about the power of creativity, the importance of entrepreneurship, and the centrality of women in shaping the future of business.

Her recognition as an industry ambassador continued to gain momentum in 2024. During that year, she was invited to speak at events that brought together leaders from multiple creative sectors, including fashion, film, and design. In these settings, she positioned beauty as an equal partner, drawing attention to its financial contributions and cultural influence. This advocacy played a crucial role in changing perceptions, ensuring that beauty was no longer sidelined as an ancillary industry but recognized as a central part of the creative economy.

Tilbury's ambassadorship in 2025 remained consistent with her earlier commitments but carried even greater weight given her established reputation. She used her growing influence to continue speaking on behalf of women in business, the importance of creative industries to global economies, and the need for inclusive representation within beauty. Her October 2025 holiday collection launch provided a natural platform to reinforce these messages. During related interviews, she emphasized how her products were designed not only to celebrate glamour but also to inspire confidence, linking commercial success with the advocacy themes that had defined her career since receiving the MBE.

Throughout this period, Charlotte Tilbury's role as a beauty advocate and industry ambassador became inseparable from her public identity. She was not simply a founder promoting her brand, nor merely a makeup artist celebrated for her artistry. She had become a spokesperson for the power of beauty as a cultural, economic, and personal force. Her appointment as MBE in 2018 provided a formal recognition of that status, but the work she carried forward in the years that followed ensured the title was not symbolic but deeply lived.

In a world where industries often rise and fade with trends, her ability to anchor beauty within broader conversations about entrepreneurship, national identity, and women's empowerment solidified her legacy. By 2025, her voice was recognized not only in beauty circles but across creative and economic forums. Her advocacy had elevated the perception of beauty from a niche interest to a respected industry, while her ambassadorship had positioned Britain as a leading player in that global narrative.

What stands out most is that Charlotte Tilbury's advocacy has always been rooted in lived experience. She speaks not as a detached observer but as someone who built a career from the ground up, navigating challenges and celebrating triumphs along the way. This authenticity gives her words weight and ensures that her role as an ambassador is not ceremonial but profoundly impactful. Her journey demonstrates that beauty is not simply about products or appearances but about the transformative potential of creativity, entrepreneurship, and empowerment on a global scale.

Chapter 14: Digital Strategy and Modern Marketing

When Charlotte Tilbury began building her eponymous beauty brand in 2013, the industry was at a pivotal crossroads. The traditional dominance of glossy print magazines and department store counters was slowly giving way to a new frontier: digital connection. Social media had begun transforming how people discovered, discussed, and purchased beauty products. For many established brands, the change was disorienting. For Tilbury, it was an opening. Her instinct to merge artistry with digital accessibility became one of the defining forces behind her success, and the result was not only a brand that thrived online but a digital movement that turned beauty marketing into community building.

Tilbury had spent years working within the fashion and editorial ecosystem, where the pace was dictated by print deadlines and seasonal runway cycles. By 2012, YouTube and Instagram had started reshaping consumer behavior. Viewers were learning makeup techniques from creators rather than relying solely on magazines.

Charlotte Tilbury biography

She recognized that digital platforms weren't a passing trend but a structural shift in how beauty advice was exchanged. Instead of resisting the change, she embraced it fully. In August 2013, the same year she launched her brand, Tilbury established her official YouTube channel. Her early videos were practical, polished, and unmistakably personal. She appeared on screen in her signature copper-toned studio, sharing step-by-step tutorials for looks like "The Golden Goddess" and "The Sophisticate," directly named after her product collections.

Those videos achieved something powerful: they turned a luxury beauty line into something accessible and human. Tilbury's delivery combined warmth, enthusiasm, and authority, creating a tone that felt both aspirational and inclusive. Unlike many corporate campaigns, these tutorials didn't feel distant or rehearsed. She spoke directly to the viewer, often using familiar phrases like "Darlings," which became part of her brand vocabulary. The videos quickly accumulated millions of views, serving as both educational content and a marketing tool that required no hard sell. The results were measurable. Consumers who might have hesitated to spend on luxury cosmetics now understood exactly how to use them, and more importantly, they felt personally guided by the woman who created them.

Instagram soon became an equally essential platform. The app's visual nature suited Tilbury's aesthetic, where image quality, lighting, and color were as critical as the formulas themselves. Her team leveraged Instagram not merely to post product photos but to construct a coherent visual world. By 2015, the brand's feed had evolved into a digital glossy magazine of sorts, blending backstage moments, celebrity transformations, and short clips of Tilbury herself applying makeup or unveiling new collections. The tone was consistent: glamorous but never detached. Each post reinforced the idea that luxury beauty could feel intimate, almost like receiving a private consultation from a trusted expert.

This approach differed sharply from traditional advertising, which typically relied on large campaigns with celebrity faces detached from real user experiences. Tilbury's strategy was interactive. She personally responded to fan comments, reposted user-generated content, and encouraged people to share their own transformations using her products. By doing so, she created what marketers later identified as one of the most successful direct-to-consumer beauty communities of the 2010s.

Her understanding of digital timing was equally strategic. The late 2010s marked a boom in influencer-driven marketing, but Tilbury's collaborations went beyond the transactional. She aligned with figures whose style and audience aligned naturally with her brand message. Collaborations with established beauty influencers like NikkieTutorials, Jackie Aina, and Wayne Goss helped introduce her products to global audiences who trusted these creators for honest reviews. The influencers, in turn, appreciated Tilbury's openness to creative collaboration and her credibility as a working artist. These relationships didn't just expand reach; they embedded her brand within online conversations that were authentic and enduring.

While other luxury founders hesitated to appear too accessible, Tilbury leaned into visibility. Her on-camera presence remained consistent across platforms,

Charlotte Tilbury biography

reinforcing the connection between her personality and her products. This personal branding proved critical to the brand's growth. By 2018, her combined social media following exceeded several million, giving her a direct communication channel with consumers across continents. When she announced product launches, the engagement was immediate. Customers interacted in real time, asking questions, posting swatches, and sharing results, effectively turning marketing into dialogue.

TikTok's rise in the late 2010s introduced yet another frontier. The short-form, video-first platform emphasized authenticity and rapid trends, often favoring younger audiences who valued relatability over perfection. Some luxury brands initially hesitated to participate, fearing that TikTok's casual tone might dilute their image. Charlotte Tilbury's team, however, recognized that the platform was shaping future consumer behavior. In 2020, the brand began officially producing TikTok content that blended product education with entertainment. The emphasis was on transformation and self-expression—core principles that had defined Tilbury's philosophy from the beginning.

Charlotte Tilbury biography

The platform's algorithm rewarded creativity, and soon the #CharlotteTilbury hashtag became one of the most circulated beauty tags on the app, accumulating hundreds of millions of views. The brand's most viral moments came from authentic user-generated videos—everyday consumers demonstrating how a single lipstick or blush shade changed their look instantly. Rather than resisting this organic exposure, Tilbury's marketing team amplified it, often reposting standout clips to official accounts. This strategy reinforced a sense of shared identity among customers who felt part of something larger than a typical brand-fan relationship.

Celebrity endorsements remained a vital component of her digital identity, but they were handled with precision. Charlotte Tilbury had long-standing professional relationships with celebrities she had personally worked with as a makeup artist—names like Amal Clooney, Salma Hayek, and Penélope Cruz. These relationships naturally transitioned into brand collaborations. When Amal Clooney wore Tilbury's products at major events, or when Sofia Vergara and Nicole Kidman spoke publicly about using her products, it carried a sense of authenticity rooted in real working relationships rather than contractual promotion.

The alignment between celebrity and brand deepened further in the 2020s. Partnerships with British actress Phoebe Dynevor, model Jourdan Dunn, and global figures like Bella Hadid brought new generational reach. Tilbury herself often appeared alongside these figures in digital campaigns, bridging artistry with celebrity culture. Rather than positioning the stars as distant icons, her campaigns presented them as women sharing the same rituals of confidence that her brand championed.

Her digital marketing model thrived on repetition with variation—a principle that kept content consistent without redundancy. Each major product line had its own narrative arc, supported by short videos, behind-the-scenes footage, and quotes from Tilbury. For example, the Pillow Talk line developed an identity that extended far beyond a single lipstick. Through YouTube tutorials, Instagram reels, and influencer collaborations, it became a fully realized world of pink tones, confidence, and romantic glamour. The consistency of this storytelling allowed consumers to connect emotionally with a collection rather than just an individual item.

The direct-to-consumer infrastructure supporting these efforts was equally advanced. From the outset, Tilbury's website functioned not just as an e-commerce portal but as an interactive beauty destination. Customers could access detailed product information, watch embedded tutorials, and even use virtual try-on tools that allowed them to visualize shades in real time. This technological integration proved invaluable during 2020, when global lockdowns forced retail closures. Online sales surged, and Tilbury's established digital foundation positioned the brand to adapt seamlessly.

Her brand's newsletters and email campaigns became extensions of this personalized strategy. Rather than relying solely on promotions, these communications often included tips, inspirational messages, and curated beauty routines. The tone mirrored Tilbury's voice—warm, encouraging, and expert. This consistency between her personal persona and brand messaging maintained trust and loyalty across a rapidly expanding customer base.

Charlotte Tilbury biography

Beyond the mechanics of social media and e-commerce, Tilbury's digital success also stemmed from her understanding of emotional marketing. Every post, video, and campaign tied back to a broader idea: makeup as empowerment. This message resonated strongly with audiences who saw beauty as self-expression rather than perfection. By framing beauty routines as acts of confidence-building, Tilbury's digital communication transcended product promotion. It became a lifestyle philosophy.

In 2021, the brand began experimenting with live-streamed events, another innovation that merged education and commerce. Tilbury and her team hosted digital masterclasses that allowed participants from around the world to join in real time. These sessions combined product demonstrations with personal interaction, blurring the line between tutorial and sales event. Consumers could purchase products directly during the broadcast, a format that proved highly successful. It replicated the intimacy of in-store experiences for a global online audience.

The brand's use of celebrity moments also evolved to fit the social media landscape. Red carpet events, once reserved for static images in magazines, became dynamic digital showcases. When Tilbury's team revealed the exact product combinations used on stars at major events like the Oscars or Cannes Film Festival, those details spread instantly across Twitter, Instagram, and TikTok. Within hours, featured products often sold out online. These instances reflected a perfect alignment of timing, technology, and cultural visibility.

Tilbury's commitment to data-driven marketing strengthened this digital architecture. Her team monitored real-time feedback, adapting product restocks, shade expansions, and campaign focus according to online engagement patterns. This responsiveness gave customers a sense that their preferences directly influenced the brand's decisions. In an era where authenticity often felt elusive, that transparency reinforced loyalty.

By 2023, *Charlotte Tilbury Beauty* had become a benchmark for how luxury brands could succeed digitally without sacrificing exclusivity. The brand's online community was not limited to product users; it included makeup artists, influencers, and everyday consumers who identified with its philosophy. The company's digital footprint spanned more than a dozen platforms globally, localized for markets including the United Kingdom, United States, United Arab Emirates, and China. Each region's account maintained the core aesthetic while adapting tone and imagery to resonate culturally.

The strategy's effectiveness was reflected in measurable outcomes. Between 2019 and 2024, the brand's digital revenue share increased substantially, contributing a large percentage of overall sales. While competitors scrambled to modernize, Tilbury's established online infrastructure and consistent communication style gave her a distinct edge. Analysts cited the company's balance of storytelling and technology as a key factor in its sustained growth under Puig's ownership.

TikTok continued to be an essential growth engine in 2024 and 2025. Viral trends around products like Hollywood Flawless Filter and Beauty Light Wand generated unprecedented exposure. Rather than producing overt advertisements, the brand focused on encouraging creators to showcase natural transformations, aligning perfectly with the platform's ethos. Hashtags such as #GlowWithCharlotte and #TilburyTransformation became recurring trends, each one reinforcing brand identity through spontaneous user participation.

Another significant development in 2025 was the evolution of Charlotte Tilbury's online loyalty programs. Customers could now earn rewards for engagement as well as purchases—watching tutorials, sharing reviews, and attending virtual events. This integration turned participation itself into value, solidifying a digital ecosystem that thrived on connection rather than transaction.

As of 2025, Tilbury's digital empire stands as one of the most comprehensive in the luxury beauty industry. She and her team continue to adapt quickly to emerging technologies, including augmented reality filters that allow users to test looks directly through social platforms. Yet the essence of her digital approach remains unchanged since those first YouTube tutorials in 2013: an emphasis on education, empowerment, and emotional connection.

Her mastery of modern marketing lies not in technology alone but in the understanding that people crave authenticity. Charlotte Tilbury's digital presence feels cohesive because it reflects her personality and professional ethos. Every post, video, and campaign reinforces the same message she has repeated throughout her career—that beauty is a form of confidence available to everyone.

This conviction has transformed followers into advocates, customers into community, and digital platforms into extensions of her artistry. In an age when brand loyalty is fleeting, Charlotte Tilbury's sustained digital relevance underscores a deeper truth: that the most successful marketing isn't about algorithms or reach, but about genuine connection built over time.

Through deliberate storytelling, strategic partnerships, and an unwavering personal presence, she has created a blueprint for how luxury brands can remain human in a digital world. What began as a series of tutorials and glamorous posts has become one of the most powerful case studies in twenty-first-century marketing—a model that continues to define how beauty communicates, inspires, and sells in 2025.

Chapter 15: Philanthropy and Social Responsibility

Charlotte Tilbury's success has often been measured in awards, market share, and the global reach of her brand. Yet beneath the surface of her entrepreneurial triumph lies another defining force: a consistent, deliberate commitment to social responsibility and empowerment. From the earliest years of her company's growth, Tilbury understood that beauty had a cultural and emotional weight that extended beyond appearance. It could inspire confidence, shape opportunity, and help people believe in themselves. By 2025, this belief had evolved into a structured philanthropic vision embedded in her company's DNA, one that married commerce and compassion with an authenticity rare in corporate environments.

Her dedication to empowering women began long before her brand achieved its global prominence. Charlotte had spent decades working intimately with women from diverse backgrounds—models, performers, and everyday clients alike. She often said that makeup, for her, was a tool of transformation not only on the surface but within. When she launched *Charlotte Tilbury Beauty* in 2013, she built the company around that ethos. Confidence and empowerment were not marketing slogans; they were central to her mission. It was a conviction that guided the social and charitable initiatives she would champion in the years that followed.

The brand's philanthropic journey formally took shape through partnerships with organizations that supported women and families. One of her earliest and most meaningful collaborations came with *Women for Women International*, a global nonprofit founded in 1993 to help women survivors of war rebuild their lives. Tilbury became deeply involved with the organization's mission, recognizing that beauty and business could contribute to rebuilding confidence and self-worth among those who had lost nearly everything. In 2019, she accepted the role of global ambassador for Women for Women International, pledging ongoing support through her company's campaigns and public advocacy.

Charlotte Tilbury biography

The partnership was not symbolic. It translated into measurable impact. Proceeds from specific product lines and seasonal collections were directed toward the organization's programs, funding training and education for women in post-conflict regions. Tilbury used her visibility to amplify their stories, bringing global attention to issues often overlooked in the beauty world. The collaboration also demonstrated her understanding that philanthropy had to move beyond simple donation—it required active participation and awareness-building.

Tilbury's leadership style played a crucial role in shaping how her company approached such causes. Her team spoke frequently about her insistence on authenticity. She believed that purpose had to be woven into every part of the brand, from product design to marketing campaigns. The result was a company culture where philanthropy was not treated as an external function but as a natural extension of the brand's personality. Beauty could be a source of comfort, hope, and opportunity.

Charlotte Tilbury biography

Her philanthropic approach found a clear expression in her *Hot Lips* collections. Introduced in 2016 and expanded in 2019 as *Hot Lips 2*, the campaigns brought together celebrity collaborations and charitable giving. Each lipstick was inspired by a different influential woman—celebrities, activists, and artists who represented strength and individuality. For every lipstick sold from these collections, a portion of the proceeds was donated to Women for Women International. The initiative raised millions over time, turning a beauty product into a meaningful contribution toward women's recovery and education around the world.

Tilbury's partnership with celebrities for these collections added both visibility and credibility. Names such as Amal Clooney, Jennifer Aniston, and Sofia Vergara lent their likenesses and stories to shades that symbolized empowerment and resilience. The campaign not only resonated with customers but also reshaped how beauty brands approached philanthropy, blending product storytelling with real-world impact. Consumers purchasing the lipsticks were contributing to tangible change, an alignment that created deeper emotional loyalty.

Her charitable efforts extended beyond women's empowerment to healthcare and community resilience. During 2020, as the world faced the COVID-19 pandemic, Tilbury's response was swift and compassionate. Recognizing the strain on healthcare systems and frontline workers, she directed her company to provide donations of products and funds to hospitals and medical support organizations. *Charlotte Tilbury Beauty* supplied skincare and comfort products to frontline workers in the United Kingdom and the United States, aiming to provide small moments of care in a year dominated by exhaustion and uncertainty. She also made personal contributions to pandemic relief efforts, aligning her brand's philanthropic resources with urgent global needs.

In that same year, Tilbury's company supported the *NHS Charities Together* initiative, a federation representing hundreds of National Health Service charities across the United Kingdom. The donations supported hospital staff and patient well-being programs during one of the most challenging public health crises in modern history. Her public messages at the time reflected a tone of gratitude rather than publicity. She thanked healthcare workers and emphasized collective solidarity, underscoring that beauty should never feel distant from humanity.

Tilbury also recognized the power of representation and inclusion as part of social responsibility. Through her product campaigns and partnerships, she advocated for diversity within the beauty industry—a sector historically criticized for its narrow definitions of beauty. Under her creative direction, her brand consistently featured women of various ethnicities, ages, and backgrounds in its advertising, setting a standard for inclusivity among luxury beauty houses. She believed that empowerment began with visibility and that representation in beauty imagery could inspire confidence across demographics.

As the company expanded, Tilbury introduced structured initiatives under the umbrella of *Charlotte Tilbury Foundation Giving*. This program formalized her brand's ongoing partnerships with charities and created a framework for long-term commitments rather than one-off campaigns. The foundation directed resources to a combination of women's empowerment programs, mental health initiatives, and humanitarian relief. The transparency of these efforts reflected Tilbury's commitment to ensuring that her brand's values remained authentic even as it grew in corporate complexity.

In 2022, she launched *The Magic Dreams Project*, an initiative that aimed to empower women entrepreneurs through mentorship, education, and grants. The program reflected her belief that confidence and financial independence were deeply connected. By supporting women in business, she sought to extend her brand's message of empowerment from the vanity table to the boardroom. Participants gained access to entrepreneurial resources, and the initiative became one of the most visible manifestations of Tilbury's broader social vision.

That same year, Tilbury continued her long-term partnership with Women for Women International, contributing funds that supported vocational training for women in Nigeria, Rwanda, and Afghanistan. The initiative provided skills training in agriculture, business, and crafts—fields that allowed women to become financially self-sufficient. For Tilbury, the mission resonated personally. She frequently emphasized that empowerment was not about charity alone but about creating sustainable change through education and opportunity.

Her commitment to philanthropic transparency earned attention across the fashion and beauty industries. Major media outlets highlighted how Tilbury's brand managed to maintain luxury positioning while authentically advocating for social causes. This dual success was no small feat. Many luxury brands struggled to integrate purpose without diluting exclusivity, but Tilbury found a balance by making empowerment itself part of the luxury experience. Her consumers did not merely purchase makeup; they participated in a culture of confidence and care.

Tilbury's approach to philanthropy also had an internal dimension. Within her company, she cultivated a workplace culture that encouraged volunteerism, mentorship, and social engagement. Employees were given opportunities to contribute time and skills to charitable projects supported by the brand. This internal alignment reinforced a sense of shared purpose. The company's human resources policies reflected inclusivity, equal opportunity, and an emphasis on professional growth for women in leadership roles.

As her brand's philanthropic influence grew, Tilbury remained personally visible in advocating for change. She delivered keynote speeches at international summits focused on entrepreneurship and women's leadership, including appearances at the *Women for Women International Annual Gala* in London. Her speeches consistently emphasized the link between confidence and capability, drawing from her professional experiences to inspire broader societal reflection. She argued that beauty, when understood correctly, was about empowerment rather than perfection.

By 2023, *Charlotte Tilbury Beauty* had extended its giving partnerships to include mental health organizations and youth initiatives. One such collaboration supported *The Prince's Trust*, a UK-based charity that helps young people build skills and find employment. Through product-based donations and fundraising events, Tilbury's brand contributed to programs that fostered self-esteem and career readiness among underprivileged youth. It aligned naturally with her lifelong focus on confidence-building and personal development.

In 2024, the company announced a year-long campaign titled *Beauty with Purpose*, designed to integrate all its charitable and sustainability initiatives under a single umbrella. The campaign united the brand's ongoing commitments: women's empowerment, diversity, mental health advocacy, and environmental responsibility. A percentage of global sales from select products was allocated to charity partners throughout the year, ensuring a consistent stream of contributions rather than sporadic fundraising events. The campaign also highlighted the brand's continued investment in sustainable packaging and ethical sourcing.

Tilbury's emphasis on sustainability reflected another layer of social responsibility. While beauty and fashion industries faced growing scrutiny over environmental impact, *Charlotte Tilbury Beauty* invested in more responsible manufacturing and packaging processes. The company introduced refillable products and committed to reducing plastic use across its collections. This environmental consciousness complemented her philanthropic narrative, reinforcing the idea that glamour and responsibility could coexist.

By 2025, Tilbury's philanthropic track record had become as defining to her legacy as her artistry. She continued to serve as an ambassador for Women for Women International, supporting the organization's work in conflict-affected regions while expanding her focus to global mental health awareness and sustainable business leadership. The brand's ongoing *Magic Dreams* and *Beauty with Purpose* initiatives stood as enduring pillars of her social vision.

Public recognition of her efforts came from both within and beyond the beauty industry. She received honors from philanthropic organizations for her contributions to global women's programs and was featured in business and lifestyle publications as a case study in integrating purpose with profit. Yet for Tilbury, the measure of success was not publicity but impact. In interviews, she

Charlotte Tilbury biography

often returned to the same principle: that confidence, opportunity, and compassion were interconnected forces capable of changing lives.

Her philanthropic philosophy also shaped how she envisioned the future of her company. She expressed a desire for *Charlotte Tilbury Beauty* to be remembered not only for its products but for its role in redefining how luxury brands could behave responsibly. In her words, the brand was about "giving everyone the confidence to dream it, dare it, and do it," a message that extended from makeup to mindset.

The continuity of her efforts by 2025 reflected a maturity in her approach. What began as personal belief had evolved into corporate infrastructure, ensuring that her company's philanthropic work would endure beyond her direct oversight. Through structured partnerships, transparent reporting, and measurable outcomes, Tilbury's brand demonstrated that beauty could operate as a force for good without compromising artistry or business integrity.

Her story of philanthropy and social responsibility underscores one of the defining truths of modern entrepreneurship: that purpose, when genuine, amplifies success rather than distracts from it. Charlotte Tilbury built an empire rooted in glamour, but its foundation has always been empathy. The countless women empowered through her initiatives, the funds raised for education and recovery, and the communities touched by her campaigns all point to a legacy that transcends commerce. In her hands, beauty became not just a language of style but one of generosity, reminding the world that the most lasting kind of radiance comes from giving others the power to shine.

PART VI: PERSONAL DIMENSIONS

Behind the global brand and the unmistakable glamour lies the woman herself — ambitious, creative, and deeply private. Charlotte Tilbury's personal world reveals the values and rhythms that sustain her success. Away from the lights of fashion shows and product launches, this part traces the balance between her family life, her enduring connection to art and place, and the persona that has become both her armor and her inspiration. It offers a closer look at the human side of an entrepreneur who built her empire with as much heart as vision.

Chapter 16: Life Beyond the Brand

Charlotte Tilbury's world has always shimmered with color, confidence, and charm, but behind the glow of her brand and the glamour of her professional life lies a private world she has carefully guarded. Her story is one of extraordinary visibility, yet her personal life remains intentionally understated. Tilbury has mastered a delicate equilibrium between public recognition and personal retreat, creating a boundary that allows her to thrive as both a global entrepreneur and a devoted mother.

From the earliest days of her ascent, she understood that sustaining her creativity required an anchor outside the intensity of the beauty industry. That grounding force came in the form of family. While her professional achievements are documented across magazine covers and business reports, the quieter spaces of her life have always been occupied by people and places that reconnect her to a more human rhythm. Her family forms the constant thread that ties her life together, offering stability amid the ever-turning cycles of fashion and commerce.

Charlotte Tilbury biography

Charlotte Tilbury married film producer George Waud in 2014, in a private ceremony that reflected the understated elegance for which she is known. Waud, part of a respected British film family, brought with him an understanding of creative industries and the pressures that accompany visibility. Their shared appreciation for artistry and storytelling formed a natural bond. The couple's life together quickly found its rhythm between London and Ibiza, two places that had always defined Tilbury's sense of self.

The marriage was a second chapter in her personal life, following her first marriage to American painter and film producer Charles Forbes, with whom she shares her elder son. Her relationship with Waud introduced a new balance into her world, as they built a blended family with her two sons, Flynn and Valentine. While Tilbury rarely speaks publicly about her family, it is clear from her few personal remarks that her children are central to her life. In interviews, she has expressed that her motivation for creating her beauty empire was, in part, to build a legacy for them—something that reflected passion, independence, and resilience.

Charlotte Tilbury biography

Her children, though largely kept away from media attention, are known to travel between her homes in London and Ibiza. The family's Ibiza residence, which sits among the island's tranquil landscapes, serves as a retreat where Tilbury can recharge and return to her roots. Having spent much of her childhood there after her parents moved from London in the 1970s, she often describes Ibiza as her spiritual home. The island's light, its energy, and its natural beauty have shaped her artistic instincts since she was young. Even as her business expanded across continents, Ibiza remained her personal sanctuary.

In Ibiza, her life is markedly different from the structured schedule of London. The pace slows, and her surroundings shift from studios and boardrooms to beaches and family dinners. Friends who have visited describe her home as relaxed but luxurious, filled with art, warm tones, and personal touches that mirror her aesthetic sensibilities. The house doubles as both a retreat and a creative space. While she does not speak extensively about her daily life there, it is understood that the island's serene environment allows her to step away from the demands of brand management and reconnect with her family in privacy.

London, in contrast, represents the center of her professional universe. Her residence in the city places her close to her company's headquarters and her creative teams. It is where much of her planning, brand development, and media obligations take place. Yet, even in London, she maintains strict boundaries between her public and private life. Her social appearances, though frequent, are almost always tied to her work—brand launches, industry events, or awards ceremonies. Outside of these, she avoids the constant exposure that often accompanies fame. Her private gatherings are known to be small, with close friends and family forming her trusted circle.

This balance between two worlds—London's professional pulse and Ibiza's calm—has allowed Tilbury to preserve both her energy and authenticity. The duality reflects her personality: a woman who thrives in the spotlight but needs moments of stillness to sustain her creative drive. Her long-term relationship with both places speaks to her ability to bridge contrast, to inhabit

Charlotte Tilbury biography

both luxury and simplicity, and to draw inspiration from each without being consumed by either.

As her profile expanded internationally after the 2013 launch of her brand, the challenge of maintaining privacy intensified. By the time she received her MBE in 2018 for services to the beauty and cosmetics industry, her name had become synonymous with glamour. The demand for interviews, features, and public appearances grew exponentially. Yet, Tilbury remained measured in what she shared. She allowed glimpses of her world—her home interiors, her design inspirations, and moments with friends—but never exposed the intimate details of her family life. This discretion became part of her brand's allure: an image of accessibility without full exposure, confidence without overexposure.

Her decision to protect her family from the public eye is not born of secrecy but of intention. In an industry increasingly dominated by influencers who build careers on personal transparency, Tilbury's restraint feels deliberate and timeless. She has stated that her focus is on inspiring others through her work, not through her private experiences. That distinction has preserved her authenticity and credibility. For her, family represents the personal core that fuels her public excellence, not a marketing extension of it.

Raising her sons while managing an expanding global brand required extraordinary discipline. Her workdays often begin early, sometimes before dawn, and extend late into the night. Yet she has made clear that family time remains non-negotiable. Even amid brand launches and international travel, she prioritizes family dinners, school events, and holidays together. Those moments, though unseen by the public, have been crucial in maintaining emotional balance. It is within this domestic rhythm that Tilbury finds the grounding necessary to lead an empire.

In the years following her marriage to Waud, her personal life settled into a pattern of private contentment. The couple occasionally attend public events together, but most of their shared life remains out of the public eye. This deliberate privacy distinguishes her from other high-profile figures whose relationships become part of their professional narratives. For Tilbury, separation between brand and home life is essential to sustainability. Her family forms the background hum of stability that enables her to operate at the scale she does.

The question of balance—between ambition and intimacy, public performance and private peace—is one Tilbury seems to have answered through structure and boundaries. Her routine reflects her belief in harmony rather than separation. Friends describe her as highly organized, ensuring that her days allow space for both creative direction and family engagement. Those close to her often remark that despite her global commitments, she remains warm, loyal, and deeply family-oriented. This side of her personality, rarely seen in media, adds dimension to her public image.

Her ability to maintain privacy while navigating fame is partly rooted in her upbringing. Having grown up around artists and creatives, she learned early how public attention could both elevate and consume. Ibiza, where she spent formative years, taught her the value of self-preservation. It is an island known for openness and freedom, but also for its retreat from the ordinary. Those lessons carried into adulthood. She built her professional identity to shine brightly while keeping her personal foundation protected.

In interviews through 2023 and 2024, Tilbury emphasized the importance of mental and emotional balance. As her company grew under the partial ownership of Puig, she continued to work closely with her teams but also underscored the necessity of stepping away from constant activity. She often speaks about how moments of reflection—often found in Ibiza—help her refocus her vision for the future. That private rhythm sustains the public energy she brings to her work.

By 2025, her family life remains steady, and her connection to both London and Ibiza continues to define her personal geography. London provides stimulation, proximity to her brand's creative core, and access to global networks. Ibiza provides rest, family connection, and creative renewal. The two worlds coexist, not in competition but in balance. Her ability to move between them reflects the dual nature of her success: professional intensity paired with personal grounding.

Although her family remains largely invisible to the public eye, Tilbury's occasional acknowledgments of

Charlotte Tilbury biography

them are heartfelt. In speeches and interviews, she has thanked her husband and children for their patience and support, noting how their understanding allows her to devote herself fully to her work. Those expressions of gratitude are among the few glimpses she allows into her private life, and they resonate precisely because of their rarity.

Privacy, for Tilbury, has become a form of power. In a culture of constant exposure, her restraint commands respect. It also reinforces her brand's ethos of mystery and allure. Just as her products promise transformation without revealing all their secrets, her life offers inspiration without full disclosure. She embodies the confidence of someone who knows where to draw the line between persona and person.

Her public visibility remains high, particularly with ongoing media attention surrounding her brand's milestones, product launches, and collaborations. Yet she continues to avoid oversharing. Even her social media presence, while active, is carefully curated. Posts focus on product innovation, artistry, and positive messages, not personal confession. This intentional curation aligns with her belief that beauty should empower rather than expose.

Charlotte Tilbury's approach to fame reveals a quiet philosophy: that real glamour lies in composure. It is not merely the shimmer of makeup or the glow of achievement, but the calm mastery of one's own narrative. She has chosen to define herself by her work rather than by the noise around it. This decision, made consistently over decades, has allowed her to build not only a business but a life anchored in authenticity.

Even as her brand continues to expand in 2025, Tilbury's personal choices remain steady. She divides her time between family life, creative direction, and philanthropic involvement. Friends often note that she finds joy in simple moments—cooking, walking along Ibiza's coastline, or spending quiet evenings with her family. These private rituals form the invisible scaffolding that supports her public brilliance.

Her life beyond the brand is not a retreat from ambition but a recalibration of it. The same creativity that powers her professional achievements also shapes her home environments. Both her residences reflect her aesthetic signature: warm, glamorous, yet welcoming. Visitors describe a sense of continuity between the woman who commands a global business and the one who hosts friends around her dinner table. That seamlessness between personal taste and professional identity underscores her integrity.

Through all of it, Charlotte Tilbury has remained acutely aware of her position in an industry that thrives on visibility. Her decision to maintain discretion, therefore, is not merely personal—it is strategic. It allows her to preserve a sense of mystery in a time when many public figures exhaust their audience through overexposure. Her approach ensures that when she does appear, she commands full attention.

In essence, her life beyond the brand reflects the same discipline, imagination, and grace that define her professional success. Marriage, family, and private refuge have not softened her ambition; they have sustained it. By anchoring herself in relationships and places that matter most, she has built a foundation from which her creativity continues to flourish.

Charlotte Tilbury biography

For all the accolades and achievements that surround her public persona, it is this private balance—between visibility and sanctuary, between global recognition and intimate belonging—that defines Charlotte Tilbury most profoundly. It is the unseen framework behind the glamour, the quiet strength beneath the glow. Her world may glitter with fame, but at its heart lies a woman who understands that true beauty begins, and endures, in the spaces the world rarely sees.

Chapter 17: Charlotte Tilbury as a Cultural Icon

By 2025, Charlotte Tilbury's name had grown far beyond the bounds of a makeup brand or a familiar logo on a beauty counter. It had become shorthand for a certain kind of modern glamour—one that merged old Hollywood allure with the unfiltered realities of digital culture. Her ascent from a celebrated artist to a cultural figurehead mirrors not only her personal success but also the evolution of beauty itself into a language of identity, aspiration, and storytelling. What makes Tilbury's influence remarkable is how seamlessly she turned her own image, voice, and philosophy into an extension of her artistry. The result is not merely a company but a cultural phenomenon anchored in her persona.

Her portrayal in media over the years has reflected both the magnetic quality of her presence and the wider fascination with how she redefined beauty communication. Her media appearances have never been passive promotions; they have been performances in confidence and vision. Whether on British morning

Charlotte Tilbury biography

shows, fashion documentaries, or global interviews with platforms like *Vogue* and *The Guardian*, she cultivated an image of authenticity wrapped in showmanship. Her familiar phrases—"Darlings," "magic," and "glow"—became a part of her public vocabulary, forming a distinctive rhythm that audiences immediately recognized. She understood that language, when paired with personality, could turn marketing into magnetism.

Television and documentary portrayals often highlighted her infectious energy and entrepreneurial drive. In 2015, she appeared in BBC's beauty features discussing the intersection of artistry and commerce, offering viewers an insight into how creative intuition could coexist with disciplined business vision. Her appearances were not scripted showcases; they were displays of the enthusiasm that underpinned her empire. She approached interviews as an extension of her brand identity, speaking passionately about the power of makeup to transform confidence rather than just appearance. This sincerity resonated deeply, reinforcing her reputation as a genuine advocate of self-expression through beauty.

Charlotte Tilbury biography

Her media presence also extended into fashion film and digital storytelling. As the beauty landscape evolved toward short-form content, Tilbury proved adept at adapting without losing her sense of theater. Her brand's YouTube and social platforms became extensions of her personality, with tutorial-style videos often opening with her characteristic greeting and ending with affirmations of empowerment. Viewers did not merely watch to learn how to apply products—they tuned in for the experience of Charlotte herself. This presence blurred the line between brand founder and celebrity, positioning her alongside cultural icons who personify their creations.

Over the years, pop culture references to Charlotte Tilbury became increasingly frequent. Her products and aesthetic were featured in fashion editorials, celebrity interviews, and even song lyrics that referenced her brand as a marker of luxury femininity. In red carpet commentary, stylists and journalists began to mention "the Tilbury look" as a visual shorthand for soft, glowing skin paired with confident color choices. By the late 2010s and continuing through 2025, this association had cemented itself across entertainment and social media.

Charlotte Tilbury biography

From film premieres to award shows, countless high-profile figures credited her products as essential to their signature appearances.

Her brand's presence in film and television reinforced that cultural reach. Makeup artists in production settings often used her palettes and lipsticks to achieve camera-ready radiance, making her name a behind-the-scenes staple. In interviews, actors and musicians spoke about her as both an artist and an icon of empowerment. The repeated visibility of her name in these contexts elevated her beyond commerce into the realm of cultural reference. She became a figure whose work symbolized success, transformation, and modern British elegance.

Charlotte Tilbury's signature personal style has been a consistent thread in her public identity, as integral to her influence as her artistry itself. Her appearance—cascading copper hair, shimmering eye makeup, and precisely defined lips—became instantly recognizable. She crafted her image not as a disguise but as a brand in motion. Her wardrobe, often composed of glamorous gowns, tailored jumpsuits, and luxe textures, reflected both old-school sophistication and modern vitality. Whether walking through a fashion event or appearing in corporate interviews, she radiated continuity. Her image was never left to chance; it was the visual manifestation of the very principles her brand sold—confidence, allure, and individuality.

That attention to image extended to her tone of voice, posture, and mannerisms. She projected enthusiasm with the warmth of a close confidante but the polish of a global business leader. When she addressed an audience, whether at product launches or industry summits, she combined humor with precision, bringing the language of makeup into the lexicon of motivation. For her, beauty was always more than skin-deep; it was a means of creating the best version of oneself. Her consistency in this message earned her a following that transcended customers—it created believers.

What separated Tilbury from many peers in the luxury industry was her ability to make glamour accessible without diminishing its mystique. She maintained a refined yet relatable presence, balancing the aspirational tone of high-end fashion with the intimacy of a personal conversation. Her branding reflected this duality: visually opulent, emotionally approachable. The result was a rare kind of loyalty in a marketplace where trends shift quickly. Consumers did not just trust her products; they trusted her persona.

Her role as a cultural icon also owes much to the world she built around her brand. Every product name, campaign, and event carried a story that aligned with her broader message of empowerment. Collections such as Pillow Talk transcended makeup categories to become cultural signifiers in their own right, referenced across social media as symbols of soft confidence and romantic energy. Tilbury's ability to turn simple product narratives into lifestyle concepts underscored her understanding of cultural storytelling. She was not just selling lipsticks; she was curating emotions.

Beyond the beauty industry, Tilbury's lifestyle influence spread into the language of self-belief and ambition. Her public statements about manifesting success, celebrating individuality, and embracing positivity connected with audiences navigating a new era of self-image shaped by digital exposure. She often shared anecdotes of perseverance—times when her determination was tested, or when she relied on creativity to overcome limits. These messages resonated in a global climate where personal branding and empowerment were central to both business and identity.

In 2019, her keynote speeches at entrepreneurial events across the United Kingdom and Europe positioned her as an advocate for creative entrepreneurship. She spoke about the importance of vision, resilience, and authenticity, echoing themes that appealed to audiences beyond beauty professionals. Her transition from artist to founder became a model case study in business publications, illustrating how personal branding could evolve into corporate success without losing human connection.

Media portrayals also highlighted her commitment to supporting women in business and the creative arts. Features in outlets such as *Forbes*, *The Financial Times*, and *Harper's Bazaar* painted her as part of a new generation of female founders redefining luxury sectors. These profiles consistently emphasized her dual identity: one part visionary artist, one part strategic leader. This blend positioned her as both relatable and aspirational—someone who achieved global prominence without abandoning her passion or personality.

As her influence extended, Tilbury's persona became embedded in modern British identity. She represented the intersection of traditional craftsmanship and contemporary innovation, traits historically celebrated in British design culture. Her brand campaigns often spotlighted London landmarks, British models, and homegrown creativity, reinforcing her role as a cultural ambassador. When she was awarded an MBE in 2018, the recognition underscored her contribution not only to beauty but also to national cultural exports.

In popular culture, Tilbury's presence continued to grow through collaborations and references. Celebrity testimonials on platforms such as Instagram and YouTube brought her products—and by extension, her image—into millions of conversations. Musicians and influencers echoed her catchphrases, and fan communities adopted her terminology, transforming phrases like "the Tilbury glow" into viral hashtags. Her appearances at major fashion events, including the Met

Charlotte Tilbury biography

Gala and Cannes Film Festival, further cemented her position as a face of international glamour.

Yet what sustained her cultural relevance was not just visibility but adaptability. As global beauty trends shifted toward inclusivity and authenticity, Tilbury consistently evolved her messaging without losing coherence. Campaigns launched between 2021 and 2025 reflected a broader representation of skin tones, ages, and identities, aligning her brand with contemporary values while maintaining its luxurious essence. This ability to balance progress with continuity kept her image modern and respected.

Her aesthetic influence reached into adjacent industries. Fashion houses often drew upon her visual storytelling for inspiration in editorial shoots. Interior design trends, particularly in boutique beauty spaces, began to mirror the brand's rose-gold palette and art-deco motifs. Even digital marketing strategists cited her campaigns as benchmarks for brand cohesion. In effect, Tilbury's vision redefined how beauty could be presented—not just as a commodity but as a cultural experience that touched multiple creative spheres.

Charlotte Tilbury biography

Public fascination with her style also translated into her being viewed as a personality in her own right. Media coverage of her appearances at global summits, product launches, and charity galas consistently noted her energy and glamour. She had mastered the art of presence—appearing approachable yet commanding attention. This command of image made her one of the few beauty founders whose personal identity held as much value as the brand she built.

By 2025, Charlotte Tilbury's influence beyond beauty had expanded into discussions of lifestyle and empowerment. She had become a figure synonymous with the idea that confidence is both cultivated and chosen. Her interviews often touched on mindfulness, ambition, and personal growth, tying emotional well-being to external expression. She advocated for the idea that beauty rituals could serve as moments of self-connection rather than vanity. This message resonated in a generation seeking balance between appearance and authenticity.

Her participation in philanthropic and cultural events reinforced this aspect of her public persona. She aligned

Charlotte Tilbury biography

with initiatives supporting women entrepreneurs and contributed to global causes promoting education and creativity. Through partnerships and donations, she positioned her success as part of a larger ecosystem of giving back. This commitment enhanced her reputation not just as a businesswoman but as a public figure who recognized her platform's broader influence.

Charlotte Tilbury's lifestyle philosophy found visual expression in her brand spaces and events. Flagship boutiques reflected her personal aesthetic—luxurious yet welcoming, filled with warm lighting and theatrical mirrors. Customers entering these environments often remarked that they felt as though they were entering her world. That immersive quality transformed retail from transaction into experience, mirroring her own personality: dynamic, expressive, and meticulously detailed.

Her influence even extended into the evolving digital beauty landscape. As virtual events and digital avatars became more common in 2023 and 2024, her brand incorporated interactive technology that allowed users to experiment with looks inspired by her artistry. The blend of human creativity and technological innovation reflected her adaptability and ongoing relevance in a world where personal image increasingly intersects with technology.

Cultural analysts often point out that few figures in modern business manage to sustain a persona that feels authentic after decades in the spotlight. Tilbury achieved this by keeping her story consistent: the belief that beauty is empowering, artistry is transformative, and confidence is universal. Her consistency did not come from repetition but from conviction. Each public appearance reaffirmed that ethos, reminding audiences that glamour could coexist with sincerity.

Her enduring appeal rests in her ability to inspire not only through products but through presence. Fans, entrepreneurs, and fellow creatives often cite her as proof that vision, passion, and perseverance can reshape industries. She stands as a reminder that charisma and credibility can coexist, and that success in modern culture depends as much on emotional resonance as it does on innovation.

Charlotte Tilbury biography

By the middle of the 2020s, Charlotte Tilbury's cultural impact had become undeniable. She was not merely a participant in beauty culture; she was a defining architect of it. Her influence spanned artistry, entrepreneurship, and lifestyle philosophy, blending seamlessly into a single narrative of modern empowerment. Whether on screen, on stage, or through the countless products that bear her name, she continued to personify the idea that glamour, when wielded with authenticity, can be a force of inspiration.

Her transformation from artist to icon is therefore not a story of image alone. It is a story of conviction expressed through creativity, of individuality turned into influence, and of a woman who understood that the truest kind of beauty lies in the courage to define one's own reflection. As she continues to shape the cultural conversation in 2025, Charlotte Tilbury stands not only as a leader in beauty but as one of the most resonant symbols of self-made artistry in contemporary British history.

PART VII: PRESENT DAY AND THE FUTURE

Charlotte Tilbury's story is far from finished. Having already transformed the global beauty landscape and redefined what it means to build a personal brand, she stands at a point where legacy meets reinvention. This part moves through her current world — from her evolving business empire and collaborations to her present-day influence in 2025 and the ambitions shaping her next era. It captures not just where she is, but how she continues to anticipate and create what comes next in beauty, culture, and beyond.

Charlotte Tilbury biography

Chapter 18: The 2020s Beauty Landscape

The decade of the 2020s brought a test unlike any the beauty world had faced before. For Charlotte Tilbury, whose brand had built its success on personal connection, in-store artistry, and the magic of transformation, the arrival of 2020 changed not only how she reached customers but how the entire industry functioned. The onset of the COVID-19 pandemic disrupted the rhythm of beauty retail worldwide. What had once been an experience defined by touch, texture, and human interaction suddenly had to exist within the limits of distance, digital screens, and shifting priorities. It was a time that required immediate adaptation, strategic agility, and an understanding of what consumers now needed from beauty.

When the pandemic forced stores to close in March 2020, Charlotte Tilbury Beauty found itself navigating uncharted terrain. The company had, by that point, already built a strong online presence, but even the most forward-thinking brands faced unprecedented challenges. Beauty counters across department stores in London, New York, Dubai, and Shanghai went dark. Makeup testers were removed from shelves, and face masks became an everyday accessory, altering how people thought about cosmetics altogether. Yet instead of retreating, Tilbury and her team treated the disruption as a moment to accelerate digital transformation and rethink the emotional connection between beauty and well-being.

One of the brand's first major responses was to expand its virtual artistry program. Charlotte Tilbury Beauty introduced one-on-one video consultations, giving customers access to trained artists through live video calls. These sessions replicated the personal touch of an in-store experience while providing tailored advice to customers confined at home. It was a move that reflected both technological foresight and a deep understanding of the brand's DNA: the belief that beauty, even in isolation, should feel luxurious and uplifting.

At the same time, the brand's e-commerce infrastructure was pushed to its limits. Online sales became the main lifeline, and the company enhanced its

Charlotte Tilbury biography

website with interactive tools. By mid-2020, Charlotte Tilbury's "Virtual Try-On" tool, powered by augmented reality, allowed users to see lipstick shades and eye looks applied to their digital likenesses. This innovation, developed in partnership with tech firms specializing in beauty simulation, helped fill the sensory gap left by the absence of in-store testing. It also positioned Charlotte Tilbury Beauty as one of the few luxury brands that could merge glamour with technology seamlessly.

Consumer behavior shifted dramatically during this period. With events canceled, offices closed, and social gatherings paused, makeup sales across much of the industry declined, especially in color cosmetics. However, skincare gained unprecedented importance. People began investing more in products that focused on health, comfort, and self-care. Tilbury noticed this shift early and leaned into it. In 2020, she emphasized her skincare line, which included the award-winning Magic Cream, Magic Serum Crystal Elixir, and the Goddess Cleansing Ritual. These products embodied the kind of ritual consumers craved—moments of calm and restoration amid uncertainty.

Charlotte Tilbury biography

As restrictions eased in some markets later that year, Charlotte Tilbury Beauty's resilience became evident. The brand had not only maintained engagement but had expanded its reach. Digital content—tutorials, product launches, and inspirational messages from Charlotte herself—became part of people's routines. Her warm, encouraging tone resonated with audiences who sought positivity. Rather than focusing solely on external beauty, her messaging centered around confidence and inner strength, aligning perfectly with the mood of the times.

2021 marked a period of consolidation and innovation. Having weathered the immediate challenges of the pandemic's first wave, the company built on the lessons learned in 2020 to redefine what luxury beauty meant in a hybrid world. Virtual try-ons were no longer a novelty; they became an expected part of the customer journey. The brand upgraded its digital tools to allow users to create full looks virtually—combining lipstick, foundation, and eyeshadow shades that matched their skin tone and lighting environment. The integration of AI into these systems allowed for personalized recommendations based on data analysis of preferences, regional trends, and even the time of year.

Meanwhile, consumer behavior continued to evolve. Many who had adopted skincare routines during lockdowns kept those habits even as public life resumed. The company capitalized on this sustained interest by expanding its skincare offerings. In 2021, Charlotte Tilbury introduced the Cryo-Recovery Eye Serum and Cryo-Recovery Mask, inspired by professional cryotherapy treatments. These launches combined science with the brand's signature glamour, presenting skincare as both high-performance and indulgent. The sleek silver packaging and cooling textures aligned with global trends emphasizing efficiency and experience.

Another defining feature of this period was the brand's growing alignment with wellness. Beauty in the 2020s was no longer only about transformation but also about restoration. Consumers sought products that supported mental and emotional well-being, a theme that Charlotte Tilbury emphasized in her communication. Her social media and marketing campaigns frequently touched on the idea that beauty was empowering—a source of strength rather than vanity. This narrative resonated strongly across generations and markets, helping the brand retain loyalty at a time when consumer trust was fragile.

By 2022, with much of the world adapting to a post-pandemic normal, Charlotte Tilbury Beauty entered a phase of renewed expansion. Stores reopened, and the brand's counters were redesigned with safety and digital integration in mind. Touchless testing became the new standard. Smart mirrors equipped with augmented reality allowed customers to try products virtually within stores without physical application. These innovations not only addressed health concerns but also created an elevated, futuristic experience that matched the brand's luxurious identity.

Technology continued to influence the brand's direction. The integration of artificial intelligence went beyond retail into product development and marketing. AI-assisted analysis helped identify emerging color trends and consumer preferences across regions, allowing the brand to tailor campaigns more precisely. Data from virtual try-on sessions also provided insights into which products appealed to specific demographics. By blending human creativity with technological precision, Charlotte Tilbury Beauty maintained a leading edge in personalization—a defining feature of modern luxury retail.

The brand's marketing strategy evolved alongside these innovations. The rise of TikTok and short-form video content offered a new platform to reach younger audiences. Charlotte Tilbury products, particularly the Pillow Talk line, became viral sensations on the app, generating millions of views. Influencers recreated signature Tilbury looks, while the brand itself used the platform to release educational and entertaining content. This digital fluency allowed the company to remain culturally relevant while maintaining its high-end positioning.

In the same year, Charlotte Tilbury Beauty introduced new iterations of its iconic products, blending nostalgia with innovation. The Pillow Talk franchise expanded with new shades and finishes, catering to diverse skin tones and preferences. The Airbrush Flawless Foundation and Setting Spray collections gained renewed popularity as hybrid makeup-skincare products, combining long wear with skin benefits. These moves demonstrated an acute awareness of evolving consumer expectations: products had to perform, care for the skin, and align with modern lifestyles.

Skincare continued to dominate headlines in 2023. The brand launched the Magic Body Cream, a full-body extension of the original Magic Cream formula, developed to deliver hydration and radiance. Marketing focused on the science behind the product—its combination of hyaluronic acid, shea butter, and vitamins—while retaining the aspirational tone that defined the brand. The company's ability to balance clinical credibility with emotional appeal became one of its defining strengths in the competitive skincare market.

Another milestone came with the introduction of AI-powered shade-matching technology on the brand's website. Customers could upload a selfie, and the system would analyze undertones and lighting to recommend the most accurate foundation shade. This innovation addressed one of online beauty retail's most persistent challenges and demonstrated how technology could enhance consumer trust.

The industry itself was undergoing significant transformation. Sustainability and transparency had become central discussions across all luxury sectors, and Charlotte Tilbury Beauty responded by reassessing packaging and sourcing. In 2023, the company introduced recyclable components in several key products and committed to reducing single-use plastics. This alignment with global environmental consciousness reflected both consumer expectations and corporate responsibility.

Throughout 2024, the momentum continued. The brand celebrated its tenth anniversary since launching in 2013, using the milestone to highlight a decade of innovation. Campaigns featured testimonials from longtime customers and collaborators, underscoring the human connections behind the brand's success. Yet the focus remained forward-looking. Charlotte Tilbury Beauty continued to develop AI-enhanced digital tools, introducing features that allowed users to visualize complete routines—from skincare to makeup—based on personalized goals. This holistic approach mirrored the changing beauty landscape, where boundaries between product categories were increasingly fluid.

By 2024, virtual try-ons had evolved from a convenience into a powerful sales driver. The technology's sophistication allowed for near-perfect simulation of textures and finishes, giving consumers confidence in their purchases. The integration of augmented reality within mobile apps meant users could experiment with new looks anywhere, making beauty more interactive and playful. Charlotte Tilbury's investment in these tools reflected her understanding that the modern customer valued both efficiency and experience.

The company's approach to AI extended into customer service as well. Intelligent chat assistants trained on brand knowledge could provide detailed product advice, mimic the tone and warmth of in-store artists, and guide users through tailored routines. This combination of automation and human touch became a hallmark of the brand's digital presence. Behind the scenes, data-driven insights informed inventory management, allowing more accurate forecasting of product demand across global markets.

Skincare innovation remained a cornerstone of the brand's 2024 strategy. With consumers prioritizing multitasking formulas, Charlotte Tilbury Beauty developed hybrid products that bridged makeup and skincare. The launch of the Magic Water Cream, for instance, offered oil-free hydration while maintaining the luminous finish characteristic of the brand's aesthetic. Each launch was accompanied by storytelling that connected scientific formulation with emotional appeal—an approach that continued to distinguish the brand in an increasingly crowded market.

The relationship between beauty and technology grew even more intertwined in 2025. Artificial intelligence became integral to nearly every stage of the consumer journey. Charlotte Tilbury Beauty partnered with technology firms to refine facial mapping and predictive analytics, offering even greater precision in product recommendations. The virtual artistry program, born during the lockdowns of 2020, evolved into a fully immersive experience using mixed reality. Customers could enter digital beauty studios, interact with virtual artists, and test complete looks before purchasing.

Consumer behavior, too, had matured since the upheaval of 2020. The modern beauty enthusiast expected personalization, ethical transparency, and seamless convenience. Charlotte Tilbury Beauty's evolution through the 2020s reflected an ability to anticipate and adapt to these expectations without losing its core identity. The brand remained rooted in glamour and confidence, yet it embraced science, data, and sustainability as essential pillars of contemporary luxury.

By the middle of 2025, Charlotte Tilbury Beauty stood as one of the few brands that had not only survived the pandemic's challenges but emerged stronger. The combination of digital innovation, thoughtful product development, and unwavering brand storytelling secured its place at the forefront of modern beauty. What began as a crisis response had transformed into a model for the future of luxury retail.

The world that Charlotte Tilbury helped shape in the 2020s was markedly different from the one she entered decades earlier. Beauty had become a dialogue between technology and emotion, data and artistry, individual desire and global identity. Through it all, her brand continued to prove that glamour could evolve with time—adapting to new realities while keeping its unmistakable sense of magic alive.

Chapter 19: Acquisitions and Corporate Milestones

By 2020, Charlotte Tilbury Beauty had evolved from a startup with an ambitious founder into a global force that occupied a rare position in the modern luxury landscape. Its rise had been swift, decisive, and largely self-driven, a reflection of both Charlotte Tilbury's instinctive understanding of glamour and her business acumen. The brand's unique combination of artistry and commerce drew sustained attention from investors and global conglomerates who saw in it the potential to sit beside the most established luxury houses. That year, the company would experience its most significant transformation since its founding—the acquisition of a majority stake by Puig, the Spanish family-owned fashion and fragrance powerhouse.

The announcement came in June 2020. Puig, headquartered in Barcelona, had spent decades building an empire that combined heritage, fashion, and fragrance under one umbrella. With brands like Carolina Herrera, Paco Rabanne, and Jean Paul Gaultier already in its portfolio, Puig had long established itself as a global leader in the high-end beauty sector. The acquisition of Charlotte Tilbury Beauty represented something different, however. It marked a decisive move into color cosmetics and skincare, categories that Puig had not previously dominated with the same authority as it had with fragrance and fashion.

For Charlotte Tilbury, this was not merely a financial transaction. It was the next logical evolution in the brand's trajectory. By 2020, her company's footprint stretched across continents, its products stocked in major retailers from London to Los Angeles, Dubai to Hong Kong. Her team had grown exponentially, and the brand's logistics, marketing, and product development required the kind of infrastructure that could support continued global expansion. Aligning with Puig provided precisely that—access to the scale and operational sophistication of a multinational corporation without sacrificing the creative independence that had fueled the company's identity.

In the public announcement, both parties emphasized partnership and shared vision. Charlotte Tilbury remained the company's chair, president, and chief creative officer, retaining a significant minority stake. This was more than symbolic; it ensured that the founder's influence would remain central to every product, campaign, and creative decision. For Puig, the acquisition brought not only a fast-growing brand but also a distinctive identity that could refresh its broader portfolio with modern energy and direct consumer appeal.

The timing of the acquisition was also notable. In 2020, the global economy was facing one of the most challenging periods in recent memory due to the COVID-19 pandemic. Retail closures and market volatility had hit beauty and fashion sectors particularly hard. Yet Charlotte Tilbury Beauty had demonstrated resilience through its established e-commerce systems and digital engagement. The brand's strong online community and global recognition made it an attractive investment even amid uncertainty. For Puig, acquiring such a company at that moment showed strategic confidence—a belief in the long-term vitality of high-end beauty and in Tilbury's proven ability to connect with consumers.

Integrating Charlotte Tilbury Beauty into the Puig structure required careful balance. The brand had always been deeply personal, with Charlotte's name and image embedded in its DNA. It was vital that the integration process did not dilute that personality or disrupt what customers valued most: the sense of authenticity and accessibility that accompanied its glamour. Puig approached the partnership with a strategy that respected these foundations. Rather than imposing a rigid corporate framework, the company positioned itself as an enabler—providing resources, logistics, and global reach while allowing Charlotte Tilbury Beauty to retain its distinct creative processes.

From a corporate perspective, Puig brought decades of experience managing luxury brands at scale. Its vertically integrated model, encompassing design, manufacturing, marketing, and distribution, gave Charlotte Tilbury Beauty access to networks that would have taken years to build independently. The Barcelona-based group had operations in over 150 countries, and this global infrastructure opened new possibilities for expansion in markets where Tilbury's presence was still emerging. The integration also gave the brand enhanced capabilities in sustainability, supply chain efficiency, and production oversight—areas increasingly central to consumer expectations in the 2020s.

Behind the scenes, the collaboration between the two entities unfolded with a clear sense of mutual respect. Charlotte Tilbury's leadership team worked closely with Puig executives to ensure the brand's tone, visual identity, and product innovation pipeline remained consistent. Unlike some acquisitions where founders step back after a transition, Tilbury remained visibly engaged. Her creative fingerprints continued to shape everything from the development of new product categories to the direction of marketing campaigns.

As the deal settled, observers within the beauty industry viewed it as a landmark moment. The partnership demonstrated how a modern, founder-led brand could enter a global luxury conglomerate structure without losing its individuality. It also reflected a broader trend—heritage companies recognizing the need to invest in agile, digitally fluent brands that understood how to engage directly with consumers in an era dominated by social media.

Puig's approach to integration was strategic. Rather than absorbing Charlotte Tilbury Beauty into a homogenized corporate model, it established a relationship akin to stewardship. The company's executives publicly emphasized their admiration for Tilbury's creative vision and acknowledged that her personality was inseparable from the brand's identity. This clarity helped maintain consumer trust during the transition. Customers did not perceive the acquisition as a corporate takeover but as a natural progression that would bring more innovation and availability of the products they loved.

Financially, the acquisition strengthened Charlotte Tilbury Beauty's position in the luxury sector. With Puig's backing, the brand could accelerate product development cycles, invest in sustainability initiatives, and expand retail presence globally. One visible outcome of the partnership was the refinement of international distribution, which allowed for smoother global launches and consistent product availability across regions. This infrastructure was crucial as the brand continued to release new lines in color cosmetics and skincare.

For Puig, Charlotte Tilbury Beauty offered an entry point into a segment that had previously been underrepresented in its portfolio. The company had long excelled in fragrances and fashion, but with Tilbury's brand, it gained a leader in high-end makeup and skincare—a domain increasingly lucrative in the global beauty market. The acquisition diversified Puig's holdings, giving it access to a younger, digitally native consumer base that aligned perfectly with the future direction of the luxury industry.

As the integration deepened through 2021 and 2022, both companies began to realize the full potential of their collaboration. Puig's operational strength allowed Charlotte Tilbury Beauty to expand more confidently into markets such as Asia-Pacific and Latin America, regions where beauty consumption was rising rapidly. Simultaneously, Charlotte Tilbury's distinctive branding and storytelling brought new vitality to Puig's overall

Charlotte Tilbury biography

image. The partnership exemplified how heritage and innovation could coexist when guided by aligned vision and mutual respect.

Throughout these developments, Charlotte Tilbury's role remained constant. Her position as chief creative officer ensured that product development continued to reflect her artistry. Each release bore her signature touches—names, colors, and textures inspired by the glamour and confidence that had defined her career. Her creative team, operating from London, continued to set the tone for visual direction, while Puig's corporate resources ensured flawless execution across production and logistics. This dual structure maintained the balance between creativity and corporate scale, preserving the emotional core of the brand while enabling it to operate globally.

One of the key milestones following the acquisition was the strengthening of Charlotte Tilbury Beauty's skincare division. Leveraging Puig's expertise in formulation and global sourcing, the brand expanded its skincare offerings, achieving consistency in quality while maintaining its luxury positioning. This phase

Charlotte Tilbury biography

illustrated the value of the acquisition: the creative vision remained intact, but the operational capacity expanded dramatically.

Charlotte Tilbury often spoke publicly about the importance of keeping the brand's DNA pure. She described the Puig partnership as a means of "turbo-charging" the mission rather than altering it. That clarity of purpose reassured both employees and loyal customers. The tone of her communications remained distinctly personal—an important signal that despite the corporate changes, the founder's presence continued to define the company's identity.

By 2023, the collaboration had solidified into a model of modern brand integration. Industry analysts pointed to Charlotte Tilbury Beauty as an example of how founder-led companies could partner with global conglomerates without losing soul or direction. The success rested largely on the compatibility between Puig's long-term approach and Tilbury's insistence on creative freedom. Both shared an understanding that authentic storytelling was essential to maintaining consumer loyalty in a crowded luxury market.

Charlotte Tilbury biography

The acquisition also influenced the brand's internal culture. Under Puig's umbrella, Charlotte Tilbury Beauty gained access to global talent networks, advanced sustainability initiatives, and new technological platforms for production and marketing. Employees experienced the benefits of a larger corporate support system while remaining connected to the entrepreneurial spirit that had characterized the brand since its launch. Maintaining that balance became a central priority of the leadership team, and by most accounts, it succeeded.

The years following the acquisition underscored how strategic partnerships can amplify impact when built on shared values. Puig's respect for creative independence and Charlotte Tilbury's adaptability in navigating a corporate environment resulted in a rare equilibrium. The brand continued to post strong growth figures, winning new awards, and expanding product categories. Its presence in flagship retailers remained consistent, and its online channels thrived, supported by Puig's global marketing infrastructure.

In 2024, Charlotte Tilbury Beauty began refining its sustainability roadmap under Puig's guidance, aligning with the group's broader commitment to environmental responsibility. The partnership facilitated access to sustainable sourcing and packaging innovations that would have been difficult for a smaller independent brand to achieve alone. These developments reinforced the brand's credibility in a market increasingly driven by ethical considerations.

For Charlotte Tilbury personally, the acquisition represented both validation and expansion. It validated her ability to build a company strong enough to attract one of the world's most respected luxury groups and expanded her capacity to shape the global beauty conversation. Yet what distinguished her journey from others was how she managed to preserve control of her vision. Many founder-led brands, upon entering corporate structures, lose their original character; Charlotte Tilbury ensured hers did not.

As of 2025, the partnership between Charlotte Tilbury Beauty and Puig continues to stand as a benchmark in the beauty industry. The acquisition has proven not to be a conclusion but a foundation for the brand's next era. Puig's long-term investment perspective aligns with

Charlotte Tilbury biography

Tilbury's creative ambition, enabling the brand to maintain its authenticity while scaling to unprecedented levels.

The strength of the alliance lies in its balance: corporate efficiency paired with creative individuality. Puig benefits from the dynamism of a brand that speaks directly to modern consumers, while Charlotte Tilbury Beauty gains the structure to sustain global growth without compromising its artistry. It is a relationship built on recognition that in the modern luxury landscape, creativity and commerce are no longer opposites but partners.

Charlotte Tilbury's insistence on maintaining creative control has ensured that every decision still reflects the essence of her brand. The colors, campaigns, and product experiences continue to echo the glamour and confidence that first captured the world's attention. With Puig providing stability and reach, she can now focus even more deeply on the artistic and visionary aspects of her role—designing the future of beauty from a position of strength.

Charlotte Tilbury biography

The 2020 acquisition by Puig was a milestone not only for Charlotte Tilbury Beauty but for the beauty industry as a whole. It signaled a turning point in how luxury conglomerates value and integrate founder-driven brands. For Tilbury, it affirmed that creativity, when coupled with strategic partnership, can transcend scale. Her brand remains personal, dynamic, and unmistakably hers—proof that even within the structure of a global corporation, individuality can flourish when vision leads the way.

Chapter 20: Recent Successes and Global Campaigns

By 2023, Charlotte Tilbury had already become a fixture in the global beauty landscape, but what distinguished this period from her earlier triumphs was the precision and reach of her expansion strategy. Her company was no longer just a luxury makeup brand—it had evolved into an international powerhouse operating across continents, languages, and consumer demographics. The years between 2023 and 2025 defined a new phase in her career, marked by her ability to scale the brand's identity without losing its emotional and aesthetic essence. This chapter traces how Charlotte Tilbury Beauty continued to grow through new market expansions, striking celebrity collaborations, and the unrelenting success of the Pillow Talk collection, which solidified its position as a cultural mainstay in beauty.

The global expansion of Charlotte Tilbury Beauty accelerated at a rate few luxury brands achieve in a single decade. Following the acquisition by Puig in 2020, the brand had the infrastructure to enter regions that were previously out of reach. By 2023, Charlotte Tilbury Beauty had established a deeper retail presence in Asia, notably in South Korea, Singapore, Hong Kong, and Japan. The move reflected a well-calculated understanding of beauty's new centers of influence. Asia's markets, particularly in South Korea and China, had become central to global beauty trends, with consumers increasingly drawn to luxury brands that fused artistry with performance. Tilbury's formulas and branding—glamorous yet rooted in efficacy—fit seamlessly into this space.

In Seoul, the brand launched its flagship presence in 2023 with a curated selection of bestsellers such as Magic Cream, Airbrush Flawless Foundation, and the Pillow Talk range. This launch was not only about sales; it was a statement of global intent. The brand incorporated local influencers and celebrity ambassadors into its campaigns, presenting a version of Tilbury's world adapted for new cultural sensibilities. Product packaging and messaging subtly reflected an awareness of the Korean emphasis on skincare-driven beauty, reinforcing the brand's dual identity as both makeup artistry and skin innovation.

China's beauty market, the fastest-growing in the world, also became a focal point of expansion. Charlotte Tilbury Beauty partnered with Tmall and JD.com, China's leading e-commerce platforms, ensuring that the brand could maintain direct-to-consumer relationships within a regulated digital ecosystem. By late 2023, Charlotte Tilbury's livestream events on Chinese platforms attracted substantial viewership, combining product demonstrations with the theatrical glamour her name represented. These appearances echoed her long-standing philosophy that beauty is transformative and joyful, and they resonated strongly with Chinese consumers who valued both prestige and personality in luxury shopping.

The Middle East continued to represent another crucial frontier for the brand. The appetite for high-end beauty in countries such as the United Arab Emirates and Saudi Arabia aligned perfectly with the brand's image of sophistication and opulence. In Dubai, Charlotte Tilbury Beauty expanded its boutique presence within The Dubai

Charlotte Tilbury biography

Mall and Mall of the Emirates, hosting exclusive launch events that blended Western glamour with regional celebration. The brand also began incorporating Arabic-language marketing materials and campaigns featuring Middle Eastern models, acknowledging the cultural nuances of beauty preferences in the region.

In 2024, the company turned its focus toward India, a market long considered complex due to its diversity and regional distinctions. Charlotte Tilbury Beauty entered the Indian retail space through partnerships with Nykaa and Sephora India, marking its first official foray into South Asia. The move came with the introduction of foundation shade ranges designed to match South Asian skin tones, a detail that reflected Tilbury's broader vision of inclusivity and precision. The Indian market's enthusiasm for wedding and festive beauty also provided a natural match for the brand's focus on radiance and glow. Charlotte Tilbury herself described the expansion as a moment of connection—bringing what she called "Hollywood glamour to every complexion."

Africa's emerging beauty markets also began to receive attention. In 2024, Charlotte Tilbury Beauty initiated distribution partnerships in Nigeria and South Africa through select high-end retailers, accompanied by online availability via international shipping channels. Though smaller in scale compared to Asia or the Middle East, these expansions signaled the brand's recognition of Africa's growing luxury consumer base and its rising influence in fashion and culture.

While physical expansion defined one layer of Charlotte Tilbury's recent success, her brand's public visibility reached new heights through a series of high-profile celebrity campaigns between 2023 and 2025. These campaigns were not simple endorsements; they were designed as cultural moments, merging cinematic storytelling with digital reach.

In 2023, the brand unveiled its "Hollywood Glow" campaign featuring Bella Hadid as the global face of its Airbrush Flawless Foundation line. The campaign's aesthetic drew on Tilbury's signature cinematic glamour, positioning Hadid as the embodiment of modern elegance. It was shot by Mert Alas and Marcus Piggott, long-time collaborators of Tilbury, and combined vintage-inspired lighting with a bold digital presence across Instagram, TikTok, and YouTube. The visual impact of the campaign helped propel sales growth in the foundation category, reinforcing Charlotte Tilbury's place in the high-end complexion market.

That same year, Lily James returned as a brand ambassador, fronting the "Magic Cream Lights Up the World" campaign. The collaboration focused on skin preparation and radiance, aligning the brand's narrative with the growing consumer focus on skincare-infused makeup. The campaign's timing was strategic, released ahead of the 2023 holiday season and accompanied by limited-edition packaging that drew attention across retail counters and online platforms.

The following year, 2024, saw Charlotte Tilbury's collaborations expand to a more diverse roster of global celebrities. In early 2024, the brand announced British actress Michaela Coel as one of the faces of its "Confidence in Every Shade" campaign. This partnership highlighted inclusivity not as a marketing slogan but as a product reality, showcasing the full range of foundation and concealer tones through powerful imagery. Coel's involvement gave the brand a fresh, intellectual edge, appealing to an audience that valued authenticity and artistry as much as glamour.

In mid-2024, Charlotte Tilbury Beauty launched another major collaboration featuring British singer and actress Dua Lipa, who became the face of the "Pillow Talk Party" campaign. The partnership emphasized youth, boldness, and versatility—traits that mirrored Dua Lipa's own brand. The campaign spanned print, digital, and video formats, including exclusive TikTok and Instagram features where Dua Lipa recreated her signature red carpet look using Charlotte Tilbury products. The visibility of this partnership strengthened the brand's reach among younger consumers who were already familiar with Tilbury's name but perhaps not yet loyal to the brand's higher price point.

The "Pillow Talk Party" campaign also set the stage for the continued evolution of the Pillow Talk line. What began as a single lipstick shade years earlier had evolved by 2023 into a full collection encompassing eyeshadow palettes, blushes, highlighters, and liners. By 2024, the Pillow Talk family accounted for a significant portion of the company's overall sales, becoming both a cultural phenomenon and a commercial engine. Charlotte Tilbury Beauty continued to expand the line with new tones and formulations that appealed to different complexions and preferences. The introduction of "Pillow Talk Matte Beauty Blush Wands" in 2024 was particularly well received, blending the brand's expertise in texture innovation with its recognizable romantic aesthetic.

In 2025, the Pillow Talk brand identity extended even further with the introduction of "Pillow Talk Crystal Dimension Collection." Released in February 2025, the collection combined the original pink-nude tones with iridescent finishes inspired by gemstones. Its marketing campaign featured models of diverse backgrounds and focused on the theme of transformation—the ability of makeup to bring light to the face in new ways. The collection's release demonstrated the brand's ability to keep a long-running product line fresh without diluting its identity.

Throughout 2024 to 2025, Charlotte Tilbury Beauty maintained a visible presence on major international red carpets. The brand was an official beauty partner at events including the 2024 British Academy Film Awards and the 2025 Cannes Film Festival. At these events, makeup looks created by Tilbury's team featured prominently in media coverage, strengthening the brand's association with luxury and artistry. Celebrities such as Florence Pugh, Jodie Comer, and Amal Clooney frequently appeared wearing Charlotte Tilbury products, often credited in fashion outlets. These appearances reinforced the brand's enduring appeal to both industry professionals and consumers.

The integration of celebrity campaigns with technology-driven marketing became another defining feature of this era. Charlotte Tilbury Beauty continued to innovate with immersive digital experiences, offering virtual consultations through its website and app-based try-ons powered by augmented reality. By 2025, the company's digital engagement strategy had become one of its strongest competitive advantages. Campaigns were not just displayed but experienced, with users able to see products virtually applied in real time. These features proved essential to maintaining the brand's connection with global consumers, particularly in regions where in-person retail access remained limited.

Charlotte Tilbury biography

Behind this high-profile activity, the company continued to refine its operational efficiency. Under the Puig ownership structure, Charlotte Tilbury Beauty benefited from expanded production capacity and streamlined logistics that enabled rapid distribution to international markets. The brand's headquarters in London remained the creative hub, but new regional offices were established in New York, Dubai, and Hong Kong to coordinate local strategies. These offices ensured that the brand's voice was consistent while still adaptable to cultural nuances.

Environmental and sustainability considerations also became increasingly visible in Charlotte Tilbury's communications. The brand began rolling out refillable packaging across key product lines, including Airbrush Flawless Finish Powder and Magic Cream, as part of its broader commitment to responsible luxury. The 2024 sustainability report outlined the brand's goals for carbon reduction and responsible sourcing of ingredients, aligning Charlotte Tilbury Beauty with the wider global movement toward ethical consumerism without compromising its luxury appeal.

Charlotte Tilbury biography

The culmination of these efforts could be seen in the brand's market performance. By the end of 2024, industry analysts reported Charlotte Tilbury Beauty among the top ten luxury beauty brands worldwide in retail sales, with double-digit growth sustained through the first quarter of 2025. The brand's digital commerce continued to outperform projections, particularly in Asia-Pacific and the Middle East. The combination of high visibility campaigns, consistent product innovation, and loyal customer engagement created a momentum that showed no sign of slowing.

Charlotte Tilbury herself remained closely involved in all aspects of brand direction. Her personal appearances at product launches, interviews, and major fashion events during 2023–2025 underscored her role as both founder and creative force. She continued to embody the ethos of her brand: empowering, glamorous, and confident. Her ability to merge personal charisma with disciplined business strategy remained one of the company's greatest assets.

The momentum of these years positioned Charlotte Tilbury Beauty not just as a cosmetics brand but as a global symbol of modern luxury. The success of the Pillow Talk line demonstrated how a single concept could evolve into a cultural signature recognized worldwide. The celebrity collaborations of 2023 to 2025 reinforced the brand's connection to art, fashion, and entertainment, while the continued expansion into emerging markets showed its capacity to meet new audiences with respect and understanding.

By October 2025, Charlotte Tilbury's empire stands as one of the few beauty brands that had managed to bridge generations, cultures, and continents while retaining a clear, emotional identity. Each new campaign added a layer to the story she began years earlier as a makeup artist in London: that beauty, when done with purpose and authenticity, can transcend borders. The global successes of these years were not the culmination of her vision but its ongoing evolution—a demonstration that glamour, innovation, and connection could move in harmony across a changing world.

Chapter 21: Holiday 2025 Collection and Future Vision

The year 2025 finds Charlotte Tilbury at a point of remarkable stability and sustained creative energy. Twelve years after launching her namesake brand, she continues to occupy a singular position in the beauty world—part visionary entrepreneur, part artist, and part cultural trendsetter. October 2025 marked another milestone for the brand: the unveiling of her highly anticipated Holiday 2025 Collection, an annual ritual that has become both a celebration of beauty and a barometer of consumer anticipation. The collection represented more than seasonal glamour; it underscored how Tilbury has mastered the balance between artistry and business strategy, building a rhythm of annual releases that are as emotionally resonant as they are commercially successful.

When the Holiday 2025 campaign was unveiled in the first week of October, it carried the unmistakable hallmarks of Charlotte Tilbury's world—luxury, light, and the promise of transformation. The packaging shone in deep ruby tones with subtle golden constellations, an aesthetic that echoed both holiday celebration and timeless elegance. The campaign tagline, "Gift Glow, Give Magic," captured her consistent ability to turn beauty into a language of confidence and joy. Each piece within the collection was crafted with the precision that has come to define her brand, merging glamour with everyday usability.

The centerpiece of the Holiday 2025 launch was the "Celestial Glow Palette," a multi-dimensional face and eye palette that became an instant favorite. It featured six new shades designed to suit a wide range of skin tones, reflecting Tilbury's ongoing commitment to inclusivity—a value that has become deeply integrated into her product development since her early days as a brand founder. Alongside it came the "Magic Star Highlighter," a luminous powder infused with light-reflecting pigments inspired by her signature backstage glow technique. Consumers immediately recognized the craftsmanship behind each formula, built from years of research in texture, finish, and wearability.

Charlotte Tilbury biography

Another highlight of the collection was the reimagined "Pillow Talk Deluxe Lip Vault," which expanded her best-selling range with two new limited-edition shades exclusive to the holiday season. The Vault became a central talking point on social media, particularly across TikTok and Instagram, where beauty influencers showcased the products in real time. Within hours of the collection's release online, the Vault sold out in several regions, echoing a pattern of rapid sell-through that has defined her launches for years. This performance illustrated how Tilbury's brand maintains a rare ability to translate luxury appeal into mass engagement without losing exclusivity.

The Holiday 2025 campaign was fronted by an ensemble cast that reflected Charlotte Tilbury's evolving understanding of modern beauty icons. Instead of relying solely on traditional celebrity faces, the campaign integrated a mix of established ambassadors and emerging digital creators, representing different ages, backgrounds, and styles. This approach reflected a nuanced awareness of the cultural moment. By blending high-fashion glamour with relatable authenticity, Tilbury continued to reach both long-time loyalists and the younger demographic discovering her brand through digital storytelling.

Behind the marketing glamour lay an intricate operation of strategic planning and timing. The launch came as the brand was expanding further across Asia, with newly opened counters in Seoul and Singapore and increased presence in high-end department stores across Europe and the Middle East. Tilbury's leadership team had refined the calendar to ensure that the global rollout aligned with both Western and Asian holiday seasons, capitalizing on cross-market celebrations while maintaining consistent brand storytelling. By October 2025, the brand's e-commerce platforms were operating in over 50 countries, supported by localized content and region-specific promotions that reflected cultural nuances.

Consumer response to the Holiday 2025 Collection was overwhelmingly positive. Reviews across online platforms praised the packaging, formulation quality, and overall presentation. Many customers commented on the collection's attention to detail, noting how the colors

Charlotte Tilbury biography

balanced festive vibrancy with everyday wearability. This duality—products designed to excite yet integrate seamlessly into real routines—has become central to Tilbury's philosophy. It ensures that each new collection serves both as an object of desire and as a practical addition to beauty wardrobes. In the crowded beauty landscape of 2025, this balance has been key to sustaining her brand's premium positioning.

Tilbury's success with seasonal collections also reflects her understanding of emotional marketing. Each holiday release carries a theme that resonates beyond color palettes. In 2025, the narrative of "Celestial Glow" captured a post-pandemic consumer mindset focused on renewal, optimism, and self-expression. Her messaging avoided overt sentimentality and instead framed beauty as a form of celebration—a language she has consistently used to connect with audiences worldwide. This approach, rooted in authenticity and optimism, differentiated her brand from competitors that often rely on short-lived viral trends.

From a business standpoint, the 2025 holiday release reinforced Charlotte Tilbury Beauty's strategic place within the Puig portfolio. Since the acquisition in 2020, the brand has operated with creative independence under Tilbury's leadership, while benefiting from Puig's global infrastructure and manufacturing reach. The 2025 collection illustrated the synergy between artistry and corporate scalability. Tilbury continued to direct the creative vision, from shade development to campaign aesthetics, while Puig's logistical and distribution networks enabled flawless execution across continents. This partnership ensured that even limited-edition products reached international markets without supply bottlenecks—a challenge that had complicated earlier launches before the acquisition.

The financial performance surrounding the 2025 holiday period further demonstrated the brand's resilience in a highly competitive market. Preliminary sales reports indicated strong double-digit growth compared to the previous year's holiday season, driven primarily by e-commerce and direct-to-consumer channels. In-store events at flagship boutiques in London's Covent Garden, New York's Fifth Avenue, and Dubai Mall attracted record attendance, with appointments booked weeks in advance. The interactive nature of these experiences—where customers could test products in immersive "glow rooms" and receive personalized beauty consultations—cemented the sense of exclusivity and participation that defines the brand's identity.

Beyond immediate sales figures, the holiday collection reaffirmed Charlotte Tilbury's cultural relevance in an era defined by rapid shifts in consumer behavior. By 2025, sustainability and transparency had become defining expectations in beauty. Tilbury's brand responded by incorporating recyclable packaging components across the Holiday 2025 range and highlighting cruelty-free and vegan formulations. While her aesthetic remains rooted in luxury, the brand's adaptation to ethical and environmental standards aligned with evolving customer values. This integration of responsibility and glamour mirrored Tilbury's belief that modern luxury must also embody consciousness.

The storytelling surrounding the launch drew on Charlotte Tilbury's personal connection to her audience. She appeared in behind-the-scenes videos detailing the creative process, explaining the inspiration behind each product with her characteristic enthusiasm and warmth. Her direct communication style—energetic, personable, and sincere—continued to strengthen consumer loyalty. Viewers did not simply see a founder promoting a product; they saw a woman who still believed in the transformative power of makeup and who remained deeply involved in every creative decision. This authenticity has been central to the enduring trust that defines her brand relationship with its audience.

By the end of October 2025, as the holiday season approached, the campaign had accumulated millions of impressions across social platforms and major online beauty publications. Influencers and journalists highlighted the consistency of quality and the refinement of her formulas. In the competitive luxury market, where new entrants and celebrity brands frequently emerge, Tilbury's ability to sustain both relevance and admiration over a decade is notable. Her brand is not built on novelty alone; it thrives on a clear, consistent vision that connects artistry, emotion, and commerce in a cohesive narrative.

Charlotte Tilbury biography

That vision extends far beyond individual product launches. In interviews throughout 2025, Charlotte Tilbury emphasized her focus on innovation driven by technology, inclusivity, and personalization. She spoke about a "beauty future" where every customer can access customized recommendations through digital platforms that replicate the in-store consultation experience. By integrating artificial intelligence into online retail, her brand aims to maintain the human warmth of personal artistry while scaling globally. This direction aligns with her long-standing belief that beauty should feel intimate, even when it is delivered through digital channels.

Her plans for the next decade of beauty are rooted in continuity as much as evolution. Tilbury remains committed to expanding her skincare portfolio, a segment that has seen consistent growth since the success of products like the Magic Cream and Magic Serum Crystal Elixir. She views skincare as the foundation of confidence—the base upon which all makeup artistry builds. Looking ahead to 2030, her team has hinted at deeper research collaborations focused on skin science, combining advanced ingredient technology with the sensorial qualities that define her products. For Tilbury, innovation must always feel human; performance should never come at the expense of pleasure.

The global beauty landscape of 2025 is markedly different from the one in which Charlotte Tilbury began her journey. It is defined by heightened competition, digital dominance, and an increasingly discerning customer base. Yet Tilbury has maintained her standing by adhering to core principles: accessible glamour, exceptional quality, and storytelling that feels genuine. Her future strategy centers on maintaining that equilibrium while leading industry innovation. She continues to invest in education and training for makeup artists under the Charlotte Tilbury Pro Artists program, ensuring that the artistry behind the brand remains visible and relevant to new generations.

Tilbury's approach to leadership also reflects an evolution. Within her company, she has emphasized mentorship and empowerment, especially for women in creative and executive roles. She often highlights the importance of intuition in decision-making, crediting her success to trusting creative instincts as much as data analytics. Her internal culture champions collaboration and creativity, qualities that have become integral to sustaining the brand's distinct voice. As the company expands under the Puig umbrella, this focus on people and culture remains her personal anchor.

Looking toward the future, Tilbury envisions a beauty industry where physical and digital experiences merge seamlessly. She has invested in developing "virtual artistry rooms," immersive online spaces where customers can experiment with products in real time through augmented reality technology. These innovations, rolled out across her e-commerce platforms in 2024 and refined in 2025, offer personalized product matching based on skin tone, lighting, and preferences. For her, these developments are not merely technological advancements—they are extensions of her long-held mission to bring the magic of artistry into every home.

The 2025 holiday season, therefore, serves not just as a commercial success but as a reflection of how far Charlotte Tilbury's vision has evolved. From the debut of the Celestial Glow Palette to the immersive shopping

Charlotte Tilbury biography

experiences and digital campaigns, the collection demonstrates how the brand has grown beyond traditional beauty retail into an ecosystem that connects people through creativity and emotion. Each product launch continues to carry her personal imprint—a combination of glamour, confidence, and the promise of transformation that has defined her from the beginning.

In many ways, the Holiday 2025 Collection symbolizes the maturity of Charlotte Tilbury Beauty as a global force. It stands at the intersection of artistry and enterprise, where innovation meets consistency. For Tilbury, every seasonal release is an opportunity to reaffirm her guiding philosophy: that beauty is not just about appearance but about empowerment. The response from consumers and critics alike confirms that this philosophy continues to resonate in a world where authenticity has become the most valued currency.

As the year gradually closes and the festive campaigns fill storefronts from London to Los Angeles, Charlotte Tilbury remains a figure of both creativity and discipline, a woman who has learned to translate inspiration into influence without losing the sense of joy that first drew

Charlotte Tilbury biography

her to makeup artistry. The glittering products of the Holiday 2025 Collection capture not only the lights of the season but also the trajectory of a career defined by vision, persistence, and purpose. And as she looks ahead to the next decade of beauty, Charlotte Tilbury stands poised to shape it once again—one brushstroke, one innovation, and one luminous idea at a time.

CONCLUSION

Charlotte Tilbury's ascent to the forefront of the global beauty industry is one of transformation, creativity, and persistence. Over the span of more than three decades, she has not only built a cosmetics empire but also redefined how women and men engage with beauty itself. Her story mirrors the evolution of the modern beauty world: the merging of artistry with digital innovation, luxury with accessibility, and glamour with empowerment. As of 2025, Charlotte Tilbury stands as one of the most influential figures in contemporary beauty—a woman whose name has become synonymous with confidence, artistry, and timeless allure.

Her legacy is not confined to the polished image of the brand or the shimmer of her signature rose-gold packaging. It is rooted in the deeper impact she has made by translating her artistic intuition into a universal language of self-expression. What began in the 1990s as a young artist's passion for color, texture, and transformation grew into a brand that reshaped how people think about makeup as a form of identity. Through her career, Tilbury has consistently projected one idea: that makeup is not a mask, but a tool to reveal one's best self. This idea has resonated globally, driving her success beyond product lines into a lasting cultural imprint.

When her eponymous brand launched in 2013, it immediately disrupted the market with its fusion of professional artistry and storytelling. Rather than relying on abstract campaigns or conventional advertising, Tilbury framed every collection around a feeling or fantasy—a "look" that reflected confidence, allure, and individuality. The *Pillow Talk* collection, which evolved from a single lipstick into a cross-category best-seller, became a beauty phenomenon precisely because it embodied her understanding of emotional connection in beauty. Customers were not simply purchasing products; they were buying into an aesthetic, a mood, and a shared sense of empowerment. By 2025, *Pillow Talk* had achieved cult status, ranking among the most recognizable and commercially successful shades in modern beauty history.

Tilbury's impact, however, extends beyond the products themselves. Her approach to business—balancing artistry with strategy—has served as a model for beauty entrepreneurs worldwide. She pioneered the idea of "makeup magic" as both a philosophy and marketing anchor, introducing a consistent, emotionally charged language across campaigns. This narrative-driven model influenced how beauty brands communicate in the digital age, where emotional resonance and storytelling often outweigh traditional advertising.

The years leading to 2025 marked a critical period of consolidation and expansion for her brand. Following the acquisition of a majority stake by Spanish beauty conglomerate Puig in 2020, Tilbury successfully retained creative control while leveraging the partnership to scale internationally. The brand's growth accelerated in Asia and the Middle East, regions where luxury beauty demand surged after 2021. By 2024, the company had solidified its presence in over 60 countries, with flagship

Charlotte Tilbury biography

boutiques in key cities including London, New York, Dubai, Hong Kong, and Shanghai. The business model combined immersive retail design with cutting-edge digital engagement—offering customers personalized experiences that blended glamour with technology.

The rise of virtual try-on tools and augmented reality during the pandemic years reshaped how consumers interacted with beauty brands. Tilbury's team embraced these innovations early, creating "virtual artistry" platforms that mirrored the one-on-one intimacy of a makeup counter consultation. The brand's virtual "Magic Mirror" feature, introduced globally in 2021, allowed customers to see themselves wearing different looks in real time. By 2025, this integration of technology and artistry had become central to the brand's global identity, aligning seamlessly with Tilbury's belief that beauty should feel both magical and accessible to everyone.

Yet, Charlotte Tilbury's influence cannot be measured purely through sales figures or brand milestones. It is also cultural. Her message of confidence, self-belief, and empowerment resonates particularly in an era when beauty ideals are increasingly diverse and inclusive.

Charlotte Tilbury biography

While many luxury brands have been criticized for exclusivity, Tilbury positioned her brand around the democratization of glamour. From the beginning, her campaigns featured models of varying skin tones and backgrounds, reflecting a vision of beauty that was global, modern, and human. This inclusive spirit has helped sustain the brand's relevance across generations and regions.

As Tilbury has often stated in interviews, her fascination with transformation began as a child growing up between London and Ibiza. That duality—between the artistic freedom of Ibiza and the cosmopolitan energy of London—infused her perspective with both creativity and ambition. The core of her work has always been about transformation, not only in a visual sense but also in emotional terms. The transformative power of makeup, for Tilbury, lies in its ability to uplift, empower, and redefine how people see themselves. This belief has remained the guiding force behind every collection, every campaign, and every innovation her brand has produced.

Charlotte Tilbury biography

In looking toward the future, Tilbury's role as both founder and creative director continues to evolve. As of October 2025, following the successful launch of her Holiday 2025 collection, she emphasized her commitment to sustainability, digital artistry, and science-backed formulations. The brand's expansion into skincare research—supported by advanced laboratories under the Puig partnership—signals a broader ambition: to integrate beauty with long-term wellness. This reflects the industry's shift toward products that not only enhance appearance but also support skin health and sustainability. Tilbury's "Skin Love" initiative, announced in early 2025, introduced environmentally responsible packaging and cruelty-free formulas without sacrificing luxury presentation. Her insistence that "glamour and responsibility can coexist" has become a defining statement in her late-career vision.

Her leadership style remains distinct in the beauty world. Tilbury has always balanced her public persona—effervescent, glamorous, and enthusiastic—with an acute understanding of business structure and strategy. She has spoken candidly about the

Charlotte Tilbury biography

challenges of scaling a brand while preserving creative authenticity. Her ability to maintain a consistent brand voice while adapting to new markets and technologies speaks to her instinct as both an artist and an entrepreneur.

As the global beauty landscape becomes increasingly crowded with influencer-led brands and short-lived trends, Charlotte Tilbury's sustained success illustrates the value of heritage, artistry, and purpose. She represents a bridge between the old world of makeup artistry—where expertise and intuition defined a career—and the new digital era, where storytelling and accessibility dominate. By fusing these worlds, she has ensured that her brand remains both aspirational and relatable.

Tilbury's legacy also carries symbolic weight for women in business. She has repeatedly emphasized that her journey was driven by both passion and resilience. From long days backstage at fashion shows in the 1990s to managing an international brand across continents, her story reflects persistence in a competitive and often unpredictable industry. In 2021, she was recognized by

Charlotte Tilbury biography

Queen Elizabeth II with a CBE (Commander of the Order of the British Empire) for services to the beauty and cosmetics industry—a testament to her influence not only as a creative but as a business leader who transformed a passion into a global institution.

By 2025, Charlotte Tilbury Beauty stands among the top global luxury makeup brands, competing directly with long-established houses such as Dior, Chanel, and Estée Lauder. Its success is not built solely on celebrity endorsements or viral trends, but on a philosophy deeply rooted in authenticity. Every product, from the *Magic Cream* to the *Hollywood Flawless Filter*, carries her artistic imprint—an attention to texture, finish, and feeling that stems from her years as a professional makeup artist. This connection between artistry and consumer experience remains the brand's most valuable asset.

In the wider context of beauty history, Tilbury's career represents a turning point: the era when the makeup artist evolved from behind-the-scenes creative to global entrepreneur. She stands in the lineage of transformative figures like Bobbi Brown, François Nars, and Pat

Charlotte Tilbury biography

McGrath, yet her approach is distinct for its theatricality and storytelling. Her ability to merge the old glamour of Hollywood with the immediacy of digital culture has created a brand identity that feels both timeless and current.

The enduring power of Charlotte Tilbury's work lies in her belief that beauty should evoke emotion. Whether through the confidence a lipstick gives or the luminosity of a foundation, she has built an empire on a universal truth—that self-assurance begins with self-expression. Her story is a reminder that creativity, when guided by authenticity and vision, can transcend industries and generations.

As the beauty world continues to evolve into 2026 and beyond, Charlotte Tilbury's influence will likely deepen, shaping not only trends but the very language of beauty communication. Her ongoing collaboration with scientists, digital technologists, and cultural creatives suggests that her next decade will continue pushing boundaries. The guiding principles she established—magic, confidence, empowerment, and artistry—are now embedded into the DNA of modern beauty.

In all, Charlotte Tilbury's legacy is one of transformation. From the backstage lights of fashion week to the gleam of her boutiques around the world, she has illuminated what it means to feel powerful and seen. Her impact reaches far beyond lipstick shades or skincare formulas. It is a story about the art of believing in one's vision and having the courage to bring it to life—glamorous, ambitious, and enduring.

Through her journey, she has not only redefined beauty but also reimagined how it is shared, celebrated, and experienced. And as she often says in her signature voice of conviction and charm, "Give everyone the right makeup, and they can conquer the world." In 2025, that message feels as true—and as inspiring—as ever.